# Oliphant's Anthem

# Oliphant's Anthem

*Pat Oliphant at the Library of Congress*

Pat Oliphant with Harry Katz

Edited by Sara Day

**Andrews McMeel
Publishing**

Kansas City

In cooperation with the Library of Congress

www.andrewsmcmeel.com

98 99 00 01 02  QUK  10 9 8 7 6 5 4 3 2 1

Design: Marcus Ratliff
Composition: Amy Pyle
Picture Editor, Library of Congress: Blaine Marshall

Library of Congress Cataloging-in-Publication Data
Oliphant, Pat, 1935–
    Oliphant's anthem : Pat Oliphant at the Library of Congress / by Pat
Oliphant and Harry Katz ; edited by Sara Day.
    p. cm.
    ISBN: 0-8362-3687-4 (pbk.)
    1. United States—Politics and government—1945–1989—Caricatures and
cartoons—Exhibitions. 2. United States—Politics and government—1989– —
Caricatures and cartoons—Exhibitions.. 3. Presidents—United States—
Caricatures and cartoons—Exhibitions. 4. American wit and humor, Pictorial—
Exhibitions. 5. Oliphant, Pat, 1935– —Exhibitions. 6. Oliphant, Pat, 1935–
—Interviews. I. Katz, Harry L. II. Day, Sara. III. Library of Congress. IV. Title
E839.4.045   1998
973.92'02'07—DC21                                            97-51785
                                                                CIP

This catalogue accompanies the exhibition *Oliphant's Anthem: Pat Oliphant at the
Library of Congress* in the Thomas Jefferson Building of the Library of Congress,
from April 2 to July 6, 1998.
    The exhibition, and portions of this publication, were prepared with funds
provided by the Caroline and Erwin Swann Memorial Fund for Caricature and
Cartoon. The Swann Fund supports an ongoing program of preservation,
publication, exhibition, acquisition, and scholarly research in the related fields
of cartoon, caricature, and illustration at the Library of Congress.
    The following objects in the exhibition are the gift of Susan Conway Gallery in
honor of the artist: pp. 15, 16, 18, 19, 21, 22, 24, 25, 27, 28, 31, 32, 35, 36, 39, 40,
42, 43, 44, 47, 48, 51, 52, 54, 55, 56, 59, 60, 64, 67, 68, 71, 75, 76, 79, 80, 81, 82,
84, 85, 86, 87, 91, 92, 95, 96, 99, 100, 105.

Oliphant cartoons created after 1980 appear courtesy of Universal Press Syndicate,
earlier work courtesy of the artist.

Cover: *The Massed Congressional Choir*, 1998. Watercolor, acrylic, ink and
graphite on artist board, 12 × 12 in. (image), 15 × 16 in. (board)
Frontispiece: *The Library of Congress*, 1998. Watercolor, ink and pencil on artist
board, 14½ × 12¾ in. (image), 20 × 15 in. (board)

# Contents

EDITORIAL CARTOONS are part of the political discourse of our democratic society. They feed on our fascination with political figures; but, if they reflect the passions of the moment, they also tell us, over time, a great deal about the history of our nation. In the hands of a master they provide insight into universal features of human nature, and make complex social and political issues comprehensible. We recognize these as enduring contributions whether the particular message pleases us or not.

Pat Oliphant is such a master. He won the Pulitzer Prize in 1966, just two years after he left his native Australia to pursue his career in this country. Today he is recognized as one of America's foremost political cartoonists and among the most gifted practitioners of this genre. He has caricatured seven United States presidents, from Lyndon Johnson to Bill Clinton, and has offered provocative graphic commentary on salient social and political issues of the past three decades. Few artists have done as much to influence the form and content of contemporary American political cartoons.

Oliphant won numerous honors early in his career, and has continued to grow as an artist. Persistent efforts to refine his style through working sketchbooks, paintings, monotypes, sculpture, and drawings from life have kept his art fresh and sharpened his commentary. With artistry and wit, he has chronicled our times, repeatedly challenging himself, as well as the viewer, with his cartoons.

Among those who have had the personal experience of being the subject of many Oliphant cartoons is the former Senate Majority leader and former presidential candidate Bob Dole, who has provided us with a thoughtful, graceful, and witty foreword. Although admittedly from the opposite end of the political spectrum than Oliphant, Senator Dole brings to the publication a profound knowledge of the issues and events portrayed in the book. His distinguished tenure in Congress and intimate understanding of, and deep commitment to, our democratic system give him a unique perspective from which to comment on the role of editorial cartoons in American political life and their important place within the collections of the national library.

Although the Library of Congress holdings include the most comprehensive collection of American political prints and drawings in existence, Pat Oliphant was virtually unrepresented until recently. Through a generous gift by the Susan Conway Gallery and an additional acquisition made possible by the Caroline and Erwin Swann Memorial Fund for Caricature and Cartoon, the Library has now acquired more than sixty original Oliphant drawings, which form the nucleus of this book and the exhibition it celebrates.

We are pleased to add Pat Oliphant's name to the pantheon of great political artists represented in our holdings and proud to contribute, through this exhibition and publication, new information about a creator whose ideas, accomplishments, and art will certainly endure.

JAMES H. BILLINGTON
The Librarian of Congress

'IT'S NO GOOD — I AM WHO I AM.'

**P**AT OLIPHANT is who he is: an editorial cartoonist who leans fully to the left but seldom loses his balance, which is important, since he carries a sharp pen. But, speaking as a conservative and an occasional target, his work grabs my attention.

What attracts millions of fans of all political stripes is his unpredictability. Surprisingly, every now and again, Oliphant sends an ink-stained harpoon off in the direction of one of his own.

While he may put a pox on all of our houses, he gives some indication of being an educable liberal. As a political veteran, I know very well how unjust it is to be forever reminding people about something they have said. But, in his own words, Oliphant demonstrates that he is politically redeemable. As for his liberal credo, he admits that he "always tried to adhere" to it but finds it "harder and harder as I get older."

Oliphant even confesses that he once voted for Ronald Reagan against my former Democratic Senate colleague Walter Mondale. He maintains that he only wanted to see Reagan elected because Reagan was easier to draw, but I don't quite buy that.

Rare is my agreement with Oliphant's message. But rarer still is my not reading him. And that is the hallmark of a first-class editorial cartoonist. To the newspaper reader, the editorial cartoon is second only to the headlines. And even then, it is the cartoon that is clipped and put on display. You don't see too many headlines framed as a wall hanging.

Humor, of course, plays an essential part in politics. I have used it during my entire career. If you are careful and sensitive, it can be very helpful. Humor can catch the attention of your audience in an instant. And, much like a good editorial cartoon, it's a picture. You look at it and the message is there instantly; you don't have to be a rocket scientist or read a five-hundred-word story.

This book reminds us of the past quarter-century of our common history as a nation—history that I have lived through and have had the privilege of being a part of. To turn these pages is to go on a tour of our times, with its many moments of drama and courage, tragedy and triumph. Yasir Arafat addressing the United Nations while cradling an assault rifle. Tank tracks over a fallen Chinese youth and his bicycle at Tiananmen Square. Slobodan Milosevic standing in a bloody field with a stone axe, thanking the world for "not interfering." And, one of my personal favorites, Newt Gingrich and me after the 1994 elections marching "off to the revolution." The Democratic donkey lags behind with his fife, complaining every step of the way.

No doubt, Pat Oliphant is one of Australia's best exports. He is central to the great American tradition of political caricature. The Library of Congress has captured a treasure in this collection of his work.

I believe he and I would get along very well. Not politically, perhaps, but personally. And that may be more important.

SENATOR BOB DOLE

**'It's no good –
I am who I am'**

February 22, 1996
Ink and white out over pencil on
paper, 11 x 14 in.

## Acknowledgments

THERE ARE A NUMBER of my Library colleagues without whose help this publication could never have been made. From the Publishing Office, Sara Day brought her formidable editorial skills and unstinting energy and enthusiasm to the project, and the book's merits are in large part due to her efforts. Ralph Eubanks fully supported the project from its inception and gave freely of his own expertise and that of his resourceful staff. Vincent Virga made several important suggestions that helped shape the book's design and content. Clarke Allen and Blaine Marshall were instrumental in the scanning and coordinating of images for the book.

From the Prints and Photographs Division, I first want to acknowledge the essential role played by Sara Duke, Curatorial Project Assistant for the Swann Collection, in accomplishing numerous daunting tasks with characteristic excellence and speed that astonishes only those unfamiliar with her work. For the first time, I had the pleasure of working closely with Linda Ayres, newly appointed Chief of the Division, who provided valuable curatorial second opinions and administrative support. I also want to thank Acting Assistant Chief Jim Carroll for clearing my path of bureaucratic obstacles. I am grateful as well to Cataloger Woody Woodis for meticulously creating dozens of records for Oliphant drawings.

For recording the interview with Pat Oliphant I would like to thank Michael E. Turpin of the Recording Lab of the Motion Picture Broadcasting and Recorded Sound Division, for their technical assistance with the scanning of images thanks are due to Lynn E. Brooks and Domenico Sergi of the Office of Information Technology Services, and for photographic services I am indebted to Marita Clance, Yusef El Amin, and Jim Higgins of the Photoduplication Service.

My colleagues and I at the Library of Congress want to thank all the people at Andrews McMeel Publishing in Kansas City who made this publication a reality, particularly John McMeel, Thomas Thornton, Lee Salem, Dorothy O'Brien, Carol Coe, and Laura Jordan. Likewise, I want to thank the staff of the Interpretive Programs Office for their hard work in bringing the exhibition to fruition, particularly Irene Chambers, Interpretive Programs Officer; Giulia Adelfio, Exhibition Director; and Denise Agee, Deborah Durbeck, Chris O'Connor, and Gwynn Wilhelm.

More personally, I wish to thank my wife, Annie Hutchins, our son, Devereux, and Charlotte Aladjem for their patience and encouragement throughout a very busy year. Finally, the best reward for me in preparing this book and exhibition has been in the opportunity it presented to spend time with Pat Oliphant and Susan Conway. Susan and her gallery staff, notably Ann Stokes, always responded to my constant calls for assistance with warmth, good humor, and perseverance. Pat takes his work extremely seriously, but himself less so, and the only difficulty I encountered in our collaboration was in the effort to create an exhibition and publication worthy of his exceptional talents. The book was greatly enhanced by the artwork produced by Pat specifically for the cover and frontispiece and by the pencil sketches that he made to represent his reactions to his own cartoons today through the medium of his alter ego, Punk the Penguin.

HARRY KATZ

# Catalogue of the Exhibition

# The Oliphant Interview

Over the course of two days, October 20 and 21, 1997, Pat Oliphant sat down with Harry Katz, Curator of Popular and Applied Graphic Art at the Library of Congress, to discuss his career, attitudes, and art. The interview took place in the Librarian's meeting rooms within the newly restored Thomas Jefferson Building, a stone's throw from—and within sight of—the U.S. Capitol. It resulted in almost six hours of recorded transcripts. For the purpose of this publication, these transcripts were edited and reduced for narrative cohesion and flow. Further revisions were made by Pat Oliphant, Harry Katz, and editor Sara Day to clarify and amplify certain aspects of Oliphant's life and work.

In the weeks following the interview, Pat Oliphant made pencil sketches showing how Punk, the penguin-intermediary through whom he expresses his personal views, might respond to these cartoons today.

**[Richard Nixon holding up his arms with the victory symbol]**

April 23, 1994
Ink and white out over pencil on layered paper, 11½ x 17 in.

Richard Milhous Nixon, 37th president of the United States, died April 22, 1994, from complications of a severe stroke. The late president had become Oliphant's signature during the Watergate hearings in the early 1970s.

**Harry Katz:** Pat, let's start talking about some of your early influences. Where did you grow up?

**Pat Oliphant:** I grew up in a city called Adelaide in Australia, a city of about half a million, I suppose. Born in 1935. Went to work at a newspaper when I got out of high school and started with total immersion on what I was supposed to do with my life, which I had no idea about, actually, because I didn't have any direction. I knew I could draw, I knew what I was interested in, but I didn't know what I was gonna do with it.

So I went to work as a copyboy for Rupert Murdoch's first newspaper, *The Adelaide News*, at a mere pittance, in 1953, late 1952. And then I moved across town after about three months to a newspaper called *The Adelaide Advertiser*, which was the competition, and copyboyed there for a while—we called it copyboy then, not editorial facilitating assistant or whatever it's called now. I was intending to become a journalist. I don't know why, but I liked to write and I liked to draw. I couldn't see how you could make a living drawing, actually, so I was gonna be a journalist.

I decided there were too many journalists and so I went to work in the art department of that newspaper; I think they must have despaired of me actually becoming a journalist and from there I "spring-boarded," if that's the word, into the cartoonist slot when our then cartoonist left to join the *News*. So I happened to be in the right spot at the right time.

All my life I had grown up being encouraged in this drawing business by my father, who—mother, too, I guess—but my father knew a little bit about drawing. He worked for the government in what was called the Lands Department, which was involved in mapping the state. He drew maps and he was a great source of pencils, paper, and watercolors—everything I wanted. And so I grew up with that always at hand and just learned to draw by osmosis.

**HK:** Were you making caricatures of your family, friends, and so on?

**PO:** Oh, yes. I was drawing all the time. I don't recall drawing my family—maybe it was too close to home. But I was the kid who could draw and, for kids around me when I was growing up, I was sort of a sideshow. Wherever there was paper and pencil around, I'd have a crowd of kids around me saying draw this, draw that. And the drawings would get bigger and bigger, and all sorts of suggestions would keep me adding to them. And these drawings—I don't know where they are now—but they were enormous things. Those kids, it was just like listening to a bunch of editors, I found out in later years, telling you what to put in these things. And maybe that's why I hate editors!

So I was a kid who could draw. I never understood why other people couldn't draw

'. . . BUT FIRST, LET'S HEAR YOUR POSITION ON THE ALASKA PIPELINE AND INDEPENDENT GAS DISTRIBUTORS!'

'POLITICS IS HELL, BEBE!

because to me it was an obvious thing; I think a lot of it is observation. I was puzzled when I first went to school and saw these other kids drawing, and they'd draw a house, for instance, so you could see both ends of it at once. And I thought, that's not right. Perspective didn't figure into their drawings and they'd all draw it the same. And so I'd draw it differently. I'd draw it as I understood it to be, with perspective and only being able to see one end of a house at a time, and so on. And it always puzzled me why they couldn't see it the way I did. There must be a crossover at some age when you're encouraged in the right areas and you take the right path and you can develop your observations. 'Cause obviously these kids didn't. They just shut it off. Of course they were much better students at other things.

**HK:** So did your father teach you perspective, or did it just come naturally?

**PO:** I think it was my own observations. Maybe that's growing up by yourself. I didn't have any brothers or sisters at that age. You make your own amusements, you know. Maybe your observations are more intense when you're by yourself. Maybe other kids who grew up by themselves didn't have the pencils and the paper. I don't know.

**HK:** Or the visual intelligence.

**PO:** I don't know if you come to the world with a full-blown ability to observe things, or whether you learn to observe things, or whether it's just curiosity, or circumstances. But it was necessary in my training, anyway, to grow up the way I did. My father could draw a bit, so he would draw things and I'd copy them, and then, too, I was copying things out of books. He also had an interest in politics and political cartooning, so he, in his own way, guided me toward Australian cartoonists. There has always been quite a strong black and white art tradition in Australia, with quite a large contingent of cartoonists, given the size of the population. Some of the best have come from there. David Low, probably one of the best cartoonists of this century—did his training in Australia, having come from New Zealand at a young age, and then went on to London earlier in the century—did the most beautiful work, excellent by any standards, today or yesteryear. And there were many other cartoonists that I watched in all sorts of publications when I was growing up. Another notable was Emile Mercier, a cartoonist with a fey, enchanted style, whose touch I feel constantly. And I guess this was all happening to me without me knowing it, but I was preparing my head for doing this sort of thing. And so I had what I think were all the right influences. I didn't know much about American cartooning, until later in the United States, but what little I saw in those later days was not impressive.

**'Politics is hell, Bebe!'**

August 29, 1973
Ink over pencil with paste-on
on duoshade paper, 11⁹⁄₁₆ x 17⁹⁄₁₆ in.

On August 29, 1973, U.S. District Court Judge John J. Sirica ordered President Nixon to turn over tape recordings of presidential conversations involving the Watergate case, rejecting Nixon's claim of immunity from court processes. The following day, Nixon released a statement from the Western White House at San Clemente, California, saying that he would appeal Sirica's order. His friend and neighbor, Bebe Rebozo, was a real estate investor, hence the allusion to "land deals" at Nixon's feet.

'AMATEUR!'

**'Amateur!'**

June 9, 1974
Ink over pencil with paste-on
on duoshade paper, 11⁹⁄₁₆ x 17⁹⁄₁₆ in.

Attorneys for President Richard M. Nixon petitioned the Supreme Court many times during the Watergate investigation to challenge attempts by the grand jury "to charge an incumbent President as an unindicted co-conspirator in a criminal proceeding." Nixon made his thinking clear when, in a letter to the House Judiciary Committee on June 10, 1974, he rejected its subpoenas for evidence, invoking executive privilege and the doctrine of separation of powers. He argued that the doctrine took precedence over an impeachment inquiry and asserted his determination "to do nothing which by the precedents it set would render the executive branch henceforth and forevermore subservient."

**'FIRST OF ALL . . . MERRY CHRISTMAS!'**

**'First of all ... Merry Christmas!'**

October 27, 1974
Ink over pencil with paste-on
on duoshade paper, 11⁹⁄₁₆ x 17⁵⁄₈ in.

Because of declining sales, General Motors Corporation announced on October 24, 1974, that they were slashing production and laying off more than 6,000 workers. That round of layoffs brought the number of workers indefinitely suspended to 36,000.

**HK:**  Pat, when did you first become politicized? Were there political discussions in the family?

**PO:**  No. There were never any political discussions. My father believed that you never discussed sex, politics, or money with anybody, and that meant *any*body, so that didn't help. I had my own thoughts about things. Of course he always voted Labour all his life. There were two parties in Australia. The Liberal Party is actually the conservatives—everything's upside down in Australia—and the Labour Party was sort of the lefties, and he always voted that way. And I guess that's where I got my liberal attitude, you might say—liberal as we understand it here, not there. And I've always tried to adhere to that, although it's getting harder and harder as I get older. I've always looked upon politics as a very boring thing. Politics itself, the nuts and bolts of politics, never interested me as much as the people involved in it. It always seems to attract a [P. T.] Barnum bunch of venal crooks. My father's credo was that there's no such thing as an honest politician and they're guilty until proved innocent. And that's a bearing I've always steered by, and it's been pretty right. Until I thought about it, I never realized that my father had planted those things in my head. But I guess that's right, he did. And it's held me in good stead.

**HK:**  Did you have strong opinions?

**PO:**  I was developing opinions which may or may not have been right but they were opinions. I was finding out where I was wrong and where I was correct. I first applied as a press artist at *The Adelaide News*. And I was rejected from there, which was not surprising, seeing I had no track record or experience. So I thought, well hell, I like the atmosphere of this place. I'll just become a copyboy and see what happens, ending up, as I did, at the *Advertiser*. And, of course, I was fairly unpracticed at anything at age seventeen, eighteen. I was just drawing in general, just portfolio drawing and maps and diagrams, and doing some casual cartooning on the side—things like that.

**HK:**  Had you exhibited any work before that or had you had any formal training?

**PO:**  No, no. Later on I attended the Adelaide School of Arts. It wasn't a very good school. I stayed there about a year and a half, two years, drawing great plaster noses and plaster ears and things in the classic way. This was part of my training as a press artist—the paper would send trainee journalists off to school to learn shorthand. Trainee artists were sent off to art school to learn drawing.

**HK:**  Academic drawings from casts. When you went into journalism, was there any sort of a

'MAY I PLEASE HAVE YOUR UNDIVIDED ATTENTION . . ?'

'IF THIS IS THE ONLY SAFE THING WE CAN DO TO GET BACK ON THE FRONT PAGES, THEN I SAY LET'S DO IT!'

seeking after truth or a desire to uncover deception or dishonesty? Was there any impulse in that way?

**PO:** I suppose so. We're all idealistic when young. Those were the days when journalism was looked upon as a more noble thing than it is now. I don't know if it carries the same caché that it did then. It was looked upon as a profession which you could be reasonably proud of. And I could see it, maybe, as a way I could combine what I could do, which was an interest in writing with an ability to draw.

**HK:** In Australia, was the route into journalism through apprenticeship rather than college?

**PO:** Yes. We had a cadetship program where you became a first-, second-, third-, and fourth-year cadet. It was four years of that and then you were graded. And in Australia, as I suppose England, too, it was a closed shop. You had to belong to a union, otherwise you didn't work, which is probably why I hate the unions. And it gave me the determination to promote cartooning as an art form, to get it some respect, because, in these union shops, a fully-fledged cartoonist was looked upon as somewhere around the same level as a third-grade reporter. That was probably resentment or jealousy on their part because we could make it look easy. And so these journalists' union gradings were not at all complimentary to my craft. The art was not thought of as anything other than a third-grade craft, and should be rewarded accordingly.

**HK:** So you were aware pretty early on that cartooning didn't get the respect that it deserved for the quality of work that it represented.

**PO:** Yes, not enough, anyway. David Low did more for the art than anybody in this century, I think. Of course there've been others, but his penmanship, and his brushwork, and his sense of draftsmanship were just so well advanced. And of course you need to believe in something when you're doing this business.

**HK:** What did you believe in at that time? What was behind the passion? Did you feel in your gut that here was a tradition that you wanted to be part of?

**PO:** Yes. And I don't think there's such a thing as a good conservative cartoonist. I think you have to have a fire in the gut to do it and that doesn't come from being a conservative. You have to, by necessity, be a liberal. Otherwise you don't get into cartooning. You go and be a lawyer, or a stockbroker. You're not gonna sit there complacently and let things happen around you or to you. It's a way of being able to participate and maybe influence. Any cartoonist who

**'If this is the only safe thing we can do to get back on the front pages, then I say let's do it!'**

December 12, 1979
Ink over pencil on duoshade paper,
11⅜ x 17¼ in.

A Gallup Poll surveying the Democrats in the 1980 presidential campaign was released on December 11, 1979. It showed President Jimmy Carter ahead of Senator Edward Kennedy for the first time in two years, an upturn that represented the largest jump in presidential approval ratings in four decades. Senator Kennedy (D-Mass.) was campaigning hard, crisscrossing the country and drawing enthusiastic crowds, but he was criticized for opposing a Democratic president when he appeared to have no issue-based reason for doing so. The poll results put additional pressure on the other presidential candidates, former Texas Governor John J. Connolly, former California Governors Edmund G. "Jerry" Brown and Ronald W. Reagan, and former President Gerald R. Ford. Streaking, the act of running naked in a public place, was a national fad at the time.

UNIVERSAL PRESS SYNDICATE
©1980 WASHINGTON STAR
OLIPHANT

KEEP THE FAITH, BABY

'WHATEVER YOU SAY, IMAM — I GUESS YOU KNOW WHAT YOU'RE DOING...'

**'Whatever you say, Imam–
I guess you know what you're
doing . . .'**

April 24, 1980
Ink and white out over pencil on
duoshade paper, 11¼ x 17¼ in.

As the Ayatolloh Khomeini and other Iranian leaders persisted in their refusal to release the American hostages held in the U.S. Embassy in Teheran, President Jimmy Carter warned on April 17, 1980, that the U.S. would impose more sanctions against Iran for failing to release the hostages, including banning financial transfers to subjects of Iran, imports from Iran, exports of military equipment purchased by Iran, travel to Iran by Americans, as well as freezing Iranian assets in the United States. Carter appealed to U.S. allies to join in its isolation policy against Iran, but most countries were reluctant to do so because of their heavy reliance on Iranian oil.

**'EVERYTHING IS UNDER CONTROL — GO BACK TO YOUR DESIGNATED SHANTIES AND SLUMS!'**

**'Everything is under control–
go back to your designated
shanties and slums!'**

June 20, 1980
Ink and brush over pencil on
duoshade paper, 11¼ x 17¼ in.

Clashes between police and mixed-race (called "colored" in South Africa) demonstrators in the depressed outskirts of Cape Town, South Africa, on June 16–18, 1980, led to 30 deaths and 174 injured. Police had banned crowds from commemorating the fourth anniversary of the 1976 Soweto race riots, but demonstrators turned instead to a commemorative work boycott. A police official acknowledged that they had "shoot to kill" orders for arsonists, looters, and other "violent hooligan elements." The intense rioting of coloreds surprised many South African whites who had thought of them as allies against the blacks.

rates him or herself as a conservative will inevitably turn out cartoons which look like book illustrations—all very competent, but with no fire or heart

**HK:** Were you beginning then to develop a reputation for being adversarial or cantankerous?

**PO:** Yes. It seems that if you express an opinion in this world people are going to call you cantankerous! I was learning to be cantankerous then. You *should* be thought of as cantankerous in this profession. It's a role you have to play, a W.C. Fields role, you know. It's the kind of public persona a cartoonist needs. I've put up with so much hyperbole from writers over the years who, taking the 'cantankerous' lead, will say this is a mean and awful person. Everybody writes the same story. So the hell with them, he said cantankerously.

**HK:** You're also, I think, considered to be a model for the angry, independent cartoonist. That public persona works both ways.

**PO:** Well, it's necessary.

**HK:** In some ways it set you apart because you're representing a tradition of controversy and conflict. Were there local people during your apprenticeship or early years on the newspaper who served you as a model of how to be an editorial cartoonist?

**PO:** I was like a sponge soaking up everything, good and bad. And then you've gotta sift it out, put it through a filter and see what comes out that can be yours. You take what you need from all of these influences. There was a very good cartoonist who worked for the *Adelaide News*, named Norm Mitchell. He had a very dynamic way of drawing. When I look back on it now his ideas were middling, I suppose, but the drawing was very dynamic. It looked as if he had just dipped the brush in an ink bottle and slung it on the paper, and there was a drawing. And it's wonderful if you can convey an air of spontaneity to the drawing itself because it only strengthens what you have to say. That's why I like to wed the two things. The drawing and the idea should fit and one should help the other. The drawing mostly should help the idea. I despaired for many years of being able to crack this and get it right.

**HK:** What, or who, began to make the difference?

**PO:** Oh, one springs to mind immediately, the English cartoonist Ronald Searle, who came out of the World War II era. He'd spent time in Japanese prisoner-of-war camps, actually making drawings while interned, at the risk of his life, and then sprang on the world in the early fifties as a terrific cartoonist, and forever remained that way. His work had a great deal

'HOLD STEADY, MEN — OUR SHOW OF UNITY SEEMS TO HAVE THEM BAMBOOZLED.'

SPEAK UP, LITTLE LADY

THE MORAL INQUISITION

'SANDRA O'CONNOR, HOW PLEAD YOU TO THE HEINOUS CHARGE OF SECULAR WOMANISM?'

of influence on me, as it did on a lot of artists in England and Australia, and here in the U.S. as well. He was, is, an absolute original but there is a feel of Ben Shahn in some aspects of his work.

**HK:** What did you learn from him? What did he show you in terms of what you might do?

**PO:** Caricature, the stretching of possibilities, the attenuation he gave his drawings—long and narrow bodies and legs and arms. It seemed to intensify what he was trying to do, just the drawing itself. I always looked at that with envy and wonder. Still do. Another influence was Carl Giles, who died late last year. There was a feeling of genuineness and authenticity about Giles that everybody loved. He dealt mostly with the nature of people, and only most obliquely touched on politics. And so I tried to roll some of that approach into my repertoire. And it wasn't the drawing alone which I found captivating, but also his amusement at the haplessness of the human condition.

**HK:** You were saying that, when the cartoonist for the *Adelaide Advertiser* went to the *News*, you were asked to take his place. So they must have seen that you could do that kind of work.

**PO:** Well, I was drawing people around the office and I was beginning to learn the essentials of caricature at that time, too. I was more or less enjoying myself and I guess they must have seen me drawing. That's why they steered me into the art department and then gave me a chance. I look back and I wonder why now, but I mean they may have seen something I didn't see.

**HK:** Did you run into any problems with your early cartoons or your editorial board?

**PO:** Because I'd been chosen to be a cartoonist at a very young age (this was in 1955, when I was twenty), they felt that they could suggest just about anything. And they did. And I felt, well, maybe they can! And so the first year or so of that sort of thing was abysmal. It was a conservative newspaper. The managing editor, and the assistant managing editor, and the chief-of-staff, and the features editor, everybody—I even expected the elevator operator— would gather about three o'clock in the afternoon in the managing editor's office. And I would submit myself to this crowd who had just come back from lunch full of claret and fine club food, belching and farting and very full of themselves, and they would, at that stage of good cheer which gave them credentials for any creative endeavor, start to hammer out a cartoon idea. They would look at my suggestions and find they were wanting, and so everybody had a hand at the forge. It was terrible. And I thought, I wonder if I'm gonna enjoy

**'Sandra O'Connor, how plead you to the heinous charge of secular womanism?'**

September 10, 1981
Ink over pencil on duoshade paper,
11½ x 17⁹⁄₁₆ in.

President Ronald Reagan nominated Arizona judge Sandra Day O'Connor as the first woman Supreme Court justice on July 7, 1981. Although described as "moderate" and "conservative," those familiar with her political and judicial records said that she was not a hardline conservative. Women's rights advocates were elated by the announcement, anti-abortion organizations were angered. The Moral Majority, a national conservative coalition organization, decried her nomination as a "disaster for men and women" and one that would "further undermine the traditional family."

this at all. And I didn't enjoy it, to the point of desperation.

Being a paternalistic crowd, they did, however, send me around the world in 1959 to study cartooning—ostensibly to study cartooning, but I think just to prove to me that the rest of the world was really there. There is a traveling tradition amongst a lot of Australians to get the hell out of Australia and get a taste of the rest of the world, then go back and, of course, be totally ignored, because that's part of it.

**HK:** Were you restless in Adelaide? How did you manage to endure it?

**PO:** Well, I knew I had to learn what I'd chosen to do. And it was the hardest school in the world because I was not only banging my head against this wall of unhelpful editors at the daily conference, but it was also, as I said, a conservative newspaper, and one thing I didn't want to do was draw conservative cartoons. It was a great frustration, so I invented this character—a penguin— about that time as a way of getting my own point of view into my work. I don't know whether they ever realized that what I was doing was trying to subvert their system and say something in my own words. But the bird became very popular and became a regular element of my cartoons. And I don't think that I ever made those editors any more liberal or they made me any more conservative. But I endured that for ten years in Australia, and nothing *really* ever got very much better because they were fairly ossified in their own position and ideas on the world, and there wasn't much room for anything else. However, in those years of desperation I had been looking around. Having already come to the United States I could see that this place was a fallow and fertile field for a different form of cartooning. There were three or four cartoonists in the country that I thought were good at that time, [Bill] Mauldin being top of the line, and Herblock, and [Paul] Conrad. In Australia we had inherited the more humorous British approach, which is born of the libel laws there. In this country, of course, and God bless it, you can say anything you like about a politician whereas, in Australia and Britain, it's possible, believe it or not, to libel these people.

**HK:** Here it's considered opinion and protected under First Amendment rights.

**PO:** Yes, and in those other places it's considered actionable. So the Brits had developed a way around that by using humor and indirect innuendo, which we in Australia had pretty much followed. I guess your styles of cartooning must be very much affected by what's possible legally. And yet, except for the three cartoonists I mentioned, and with all these wonderful First Amendment guarantees, cartooning was a stagnating tradition in this country. It wasn't vibrant at all. It had been reduced to a series of symbols—doves all over the bloody place,

---

**'Sí, Presidente Duarte, you can tell them in Washington that El Salvador continues to move steadily towards democracy.'**

September 24, 1981
Ink over pencil on duoshade paper, 11⁹⁄₁₆ x 17⅝ in.

Salvadoran President Jose Napoleon Duarte spent ten days in September 1981 touring the United States, during which he visited with President Ronald Reagan and other officials in Washington and addressed the United Nations. He worked to build U.S. support for his government as well as to obtain economic and military assistance against leftist guerilla forces in El Salvador. In response to a question by Vice President George Bush about reported acts of violence against Salvadoran citizens, Duarte said that his government had dismissed 600 National Guardsmen and imprisoned another 64 for crimes against civilians. Congressional leaders remained skeptical about Duarte's claims to have curtailed human rights abuses.

'SI, PRESIDENTE DUARTE, YOU CAN TELL THEM IN WASHINGTON THAT EL SALVADOR CONTINUES TO MOVE STEADILY TOWARDS DEMOCRACY.'

ALLIANCE FOR SOME SORT OF PROGRESS

labeled "peace." Scrolls in their mouths and Hope coming over the hill, and all this stuff, and the Rocky Road to Prosperity, labeled, of course. So the whole thing was, you know, . . . .

**HK:** Too clichéd, too many clichés and symbols?

**PO:** Yes, and with nothing much to say. Then, of course, in later years, when I studied the American scene a bit more, I realized there was a whole bunch of cartoonists that had been eclipsed and forgotten. On looking back, the fifties were very repressive times. And now we've come full circle. We're back to political correctness. I feel like I'm back in the fifties in Australia.

**HK:** Let's move on to around 1964, you're looking for a new situation.

**PO:** Well I was looking around long before that, as I said.

**HK:** Were you looking in Australia, or England?

**PO:** No, everybody went to England. I couldn't understand why. They were just going back into the fire, you know. So, no, I wanted to come here. I could see all sorts of possibilities in this country. And, to my mind, everything was happening in the sixties here, and, naturally, I wanted to be where it was happening. All of the civil rights upheavals were going on. And in Australia nothing was happening.

**HK:** So, how did you find out about the job in Denver?

**PO:** I sent my work off to a whole bunch of newspapers, everything from the *New York Times* to the *Desert Sun* in Nevada. One evening, an American friend of mine, who was in Adelaide advising on our traffic congestion, drew my attention to a *Time* magazine story. Conrad had left the *Denver Post*, the story said, and gone to the *Los Angeles Times*. So I sent my stuff to Denver. By then they had looked at about eighty domestic applicants. Palmer Hoyt was the publisher at the *Post*, a very gruff and colorful fellow who had narcolepsy. This is a later story, but we'd be gathered around his desk and he would be discussing things of seemingly great importance with the editorial staff, and be cleaning his ear with a Q-tip at the same time, and would then fall asleep with the Q-tip still in his ear.

**HK:** Great material for a cartoon!

**PO:** I thought, this is more like it! This is a newspaper I can live with! And so, about the time I sent them my material, Palmer Hoyt had discarded the idea of getting a cartoonist. He said, screw it, we'll just buy from a syndicate, we won't get a cartoonist at all. The editorial

**Alliance for some sort of progress**

February 26, 1982
Ink and white out over pencil on layered paper, 11¼ x 17½ in.

The United Auto Workers (UAW) and Ford Motor Company tentatively agreed on February 13, 1982, to a new labor contract that included concessions on wages and benefits in return for job security. Rank-and-file members approved the contract on February 17. The persistent slump in Ford car sales, more than $1 billion in losses, and the reality of 55,000 workers on indefinite layoff had led to the accommodation. The rising sun toward which management and labor are limping together refers to increased competition from Japanese automakers.

page deputy editor said, well let's try this guy from Australia. And Hoyt said, I don't want to do that. And this guy, by name of Jim Idema, said, well, you know he's coming here anyway. I had, at that time, got all my immigration papers together, and I was coming, job or no job. And he said, he's paying his own way, for himself and his family and everything, so why don't we just try him out? So Palmer Hoyt said, in his way, well, okay, dammit.

So I ended up in Denver. I left work in Adelaide on the Friday and started work in Denver on the following Monday. And I looked out the window on that Monday morning and I thought, JEEESUS, what have I done?

**HK:** Well, what had you done? I mean, what was the editorial situation like?

**PO:** Well, the political situation was great. This was Johnson-Goldwater campaign time, and I really thought I'd died and gone to heaven. 'Cause, you know, when things got slow in Australia, and that was a lot of the time, I'd end up drawing a weather cartoon. We had great opinions at the *Advertiser*, you know. We were very fearless in our opinions of the weather. Good weather was good, and bad weather was bad and, by God, we came down foursquare and hard against bad weather. And then, suddenly, I was in a place where I didn't have to ever do that again . . . .

**HK:** What appealed to you about Denver?

**PO:** Oh, it was just the feeling of it, the thrill of being in a new place and picking up new stuff. Being in, as what I thought of it, the middle of things, you know, Denver in 1964. The campaigns traveling through. It was a circus. It was wonderful. It was a cornucopia of material. So much to work with every day. There was all this subject matter . . . .

**HK:** And what role did the editorial board play at that point? I mean, what kind of freedom did you have that you didn't have, maybe, in Adelaide?

**PO:** Well, you know, wherever you go you've got to train editors. Especially in your younger years, they need to be brought to realize that you've got some ideas of your own and it's your name that goes on it. Therefore, you've got to have input yourself. And they left me pretty much alone. Palmer Hoyt, however, was a friend of Lyndon Johnson and that gave us some awkward moments, as will happen anywhere when a cozy publisher-politician relationship exists.

**HK:** So you had some run-ins early on. What was your relationship with the editors?

**PO:** It was good. It was never the tiresome thing that I'd experienced in Australia. It was

**Watchdog**

December 21, 1982
Ink over pencil on layered paper,
11¼ x 17½ in.

The Environmental Protection Agency (EPA) identified 418 hazardous waste dumps on December 20, 1982, as priorities for the five-year "Superfund" nationwide cleanup enacted by Congress in 1980. EPA Administrator Anne M. Gorsuch also announced that the agency might not seek continuation of the federal cleanup following expiration of the current legislation in 1985. She had earlier been cited for contempt for refusing to submit subpoenaed information concerning enforcement of the superfund law. The Supreme Court, at the request of the Reagan administration, declared the contempt citation unconstiutional. Representative James J. Florio of New Jersey, one of the authors of the superfund law, denounced the EPA's actions toward cleanup as abysmal.

WATCHDOG

good give and take. I never again experienced the suppression that I had in Australia. Bad as things might get, they never were as bad as they were back there. I was grateful and happy to be here. And then, after I'd been here a year, I won the Pulitzer, and that's another story.

**HK:** Did your Australian background give you an outsider's advantage?

**PO:** I think an outsider's point of view is always handy. But I've been here thirty-three years now and I have to be careful to maintain an outsider's point of view. I'm a citizen. I like living here. I feel like part of the country. It wasn't a big culture shock to come here because of all the reading and TV material we were exposed to in Australia. Most of the magazines—*Time*, *Life*, *Newsweek*, *Look*, etc.—everything originated in this country. Even if you go to Australia today it's very much like visiting a state you haven't been to.

**HK:** They were new faces, but were they new issues that you were dealing with?

**PO:** It was a kaleidoscope of issues, civil rights being the big thing, close up, and then developing into Vietnam. And this was the introduction of the Great Society. Of course, we didn't know what a mishmash that would become at the time. It looked like the good and proper thing to do. So Goldwater was clearly the bad guy, although, when I met him in later years, he wasn't a bad guy at all! So from that I learned you mustn't meet politicians. It's too easy to start liking them.

**HK:** Okay, Pat, let's talk a little bit about the situation you came into in Denver. Paul Conrad had left and gone to the *L.A. Times*. Although it was early in his career, he was developing a reputation for independent-mindedness himself, and strong cartooning. And you're moving into that position. What do you think were the expectations? Did his example make it easier for you to work with the editorial board?

**PO:** Certainly he made it a little simpler, I think. At least they'd been schooled in the handling of an independent-minded cartoonist. They knew what to expect—at least a little bit of what to expect—having dealt with him. My expectations were unlimited. I thought, well, I've come from one end of the spectrum and the planet to the other—I can do anything I like now. It worked out as being somewhere in the middle. But it was far better than what I had before, and it lived up to my every expectation.

**HK:** Was there a sense at the *Denver Post* that they were trying to produce high-quality editorial cartoons, and that that was important?

**[U.S. Embassy – Business as usual]**

April 20, 1983
Ink over pencil on layered paper, 11¼ x 17½ in.

At midday on April 18, 1983, a massive car-bomb reduced the U.S. embassy in Beirut, Lebanon, to rubble, killing dozens and wounding over one hundred. Casualties included U.S. staff members, Marine guards, Lebanese clerical workers and civilians. Congressmen urged the U.S. to end its military presence in Lebanon – talks had, in fact, been underway for the withdrawal of U.S. and Israeli forces from Lebanon. President Reagan denounced the terrorist attack, saying it would not deter the U.S. from its goals in the region.

**PO:** They were, by my reckoning, absolutely open to it. And I found that what I loved about this country was the welcoming nature of Americans themselves. The audience was so different from that in Australia. Australia suffers—having inherited it from Britain, I think—from the tall poppy syndrome, where nobody should be successful. And if you are, you're going to get cut off at the neck or the knees. You must not be enthusiastic about anything or toward any person. Any notable or admirable achievement should be let pass without acknowledgment, if possible. That's what I grew up with, so I came here to escape, and my expectations were more than met by the American audience, which is just so open and accepting. Of course, I got my share of cartoons coming back scrawled with crayon, "If you don't like it here, why don't you go back where you came from?" The one sentence sort of things, you know. And, of course, with no return address. But not much of that at all. I was just overwhelmed, really, by the acceptance.

**HK:** Well, within a year or so of when you got here, in 1966, you were awarded the Pulitzer Prize. Can you tell us about that? That's very early acceptance. What did that mean? What were the circumstances of the competition?

**PO:** I had some nagging misgivings about it, unfortunately. I'd like to have enjoyed winning the Pulitzer more than I did. I was beginning to get a jaundiced idea of prizes, what they went for, who gave them, who got them. The year before I entered this Pulitzer thing, I'd come upon a book in the library, and it had all the Pulitzer prizewinning cartoons from the beginning, up until about five years before. I forget the name of the book [Gerald W. Johnson, *The Lines are Drawn*, 1958], but I noticed that, apart from those by Mauldin and Herblock, all these cartoons had a certain note to them. They were obviously jingoistic, rather insular, and not too well expressed. And some were so bad that even an editor shouldn't have liked them. When you enter the Pulitzer, you submit, I think, twelve cartoons, which is wrong in itself. I have a problem with that. Twelve cartoons to represent and typify your entire year's work. You submit those twelve to the people at Columbia [University School of Journalism], and that's it.

Well, I submitted eleven cartoons that I liked, but I also had committed a cartoon during that year which could have typified all the bad cartoons I saw in that book. After I'd drawn it, I'd gone home not feeling particularly good about it and, when I saw it the next morning, some nitwit editor, seeking to improve the work, had changed the caption on it overnight, without, of course, referring to me. Anyway, I thought, that's the sort of cartoon these people like. We'll see. So my entry for the Pulitzer that year was a collection of eleven cartoons I liked and one I didn't like at all. Sure enough, I won the Pulitzer Prize, and the one cartoon

"THEY WON'T GET US TO THE CONFERENCE TABLE . . . WILL THEY?"

THERE HE GOES AGAIN.

they picked to typify my work was this wretched thing. It was a dichotomous feeling. I'd won the Pulitzer. Wow! I'd been here a year-and-a-half, two years, and, the way I felt about it, I'd won it for the wrong reason. It wasn't a good feeling. When you win the Pulitzer Prize, you're supposed to go to Macalester College in St. Paul, and tell them how you won the Pulitzer Prize. So I did. And I haven't heard from the Pulitzer committee since, and I never expect to hear from them again.

**HK:** Hoist with your own petard?

**PO:** No, I hoist *them* with their own petard, or so I considered it. I felt I'd made some sort of comment on prizes in general that needed to be made, and so I had the very mixed feeling of having won the Pulitzer two years after I'd come here and then feeling this was a very mixed bag.

**HK:** A hollow victory of sorts.

**PO:** Pyrrhic.

**HK:** Pyrrhic in the sense of what you were giving up? You were getting the recognition.

**PO:** Well, Pyrrhic victories cost more than they gain, so perhaps that's not a correct characterization. I could have *not* admitted it. I could have just accepted it and said nothing. But I couldn't do that, feeling the way I did. What I did gain from winning, however, was the right to criticize the process. I was aware, having talked to Bill Mauldin some time beforehand, that these prizes aren't all they're cracked up to be, especially the Pulitzer. He believed, and I believed, and believe, that political awards are passed under the table by editors to editors within the committees of the Pulitzer. They pass these things around. You give me one this year, I'll give you one next year. I'll give you this on that category, you give me this on that. I did have, coincidentally, an editor or two of mine who were on the committees that year, so it seemed to indicate that the fix was in for the Pulitzer. To illustrate the point, a couple of years earlier, Mauldin drew, the afternoon Kennedy was shot, the 'weeping Lincoln' cartoon, so-called, which is arguably the finest piece of editorial art drawn in this half of this century. For drawing, for expression, for execution under deadline it met all the criteria for a Pulitzer. Naturally, it didn't win. It fell to politics.

**HK:** Because it's not just the cartoonist who gains the glory, it's also the newspaper?

**PO:** It's the newspaper, yes, absolutely. So the newspapers are real believers in this award.

**There he goes again.**

February 8, 1984
Ink over pencil on layered paper,
11³⁄₁₆ x 17½ in.

President Ronald Reagan opened his campaign for a second term on January 30, 1984, making education and the deficit his principal issues. In his weekly radio broadcast on February 4, he accused the Democrats of attacking his call for a bipartisan effort to reduce the deficit, and, in a speech before a Republican crowd in Las Vegas on February 7, he accused his Democratic predecessors of having "ravaged" the nation with inflation. Earlier that day, he addressed a national meeting of secondary school principals in which he claimed to have put education at the top of the American agenda, producing a grassroots revolution. "There he goes again," is a reference to a favorite Reagan putdown in presidential campaign debates, and to Reagan's own reputation as the "Teflon president," to whom nothing stuck.

LET A THOUSAND FLOWERS BLOOM.

**Let a thousand flowers bloom.**

March 25, 1986
Ink and white out over pencil on
layered paper, 11⁵⁄₁₆ x 17⁹⁄₁₆ in.

On March 23, 1986, a huge U.S. Navy task force gathered in the Mediterranean Sea off the coast of Libya to conduct "freedom of navigation" exercises in the disputed waters of the Gulf of Sidra. When Libya fired missiles at American warplanes, the United States responded by attacking Libyan ships and a missile installation on the mainland. Most commentators feared that the action would backfire, giving Libyan leader Colonel Muammer el-Qaddafi an opportunity to "stand up" to the U.S. and enhance his prestige at home and in the Arab world. In his response to American hostilities on March 25, Qaddafi stated, "This is not the time for speaking. It is a time for confrontation, for war."

**[Watch my lips – I'm gonna be the <u>environment</u> president!]**

December 7, 1988
Ink and white out over pencil on paper,
11½ x 17¹⁄₁₆ in.

President-elect George Bush met with a group of leading environmentalists on November 30, 1988, having declared during his campaign "I am an environmentalist." Most major environmental groups had faulted his record on the environment, however, and had supported the Democratic presidential candidate Michael Dukakis. While speaking at a news conference on December 6, Bush's appointee for chairman of the White House Council of Economic Advisers, Michael J. Boskin, endorsed Bush's pledge to bring the deficit under control without a tax increase. This should be done, he said, by slowing the growth in government spending. Bush had brought down the house at the Republican convention in August with his proclamation, "Read my lips – No new taxes!"

43

And I'd like to have believed in it myself but I just couldn't. In ensuing years, I've sent the committee angry telegrams, votes of no confidence when I've disagreed with them. One year, during Watergate, the Pulitzer committee, in its wisdom, at a time when even bad cartoonists were doing good cartoons, decided that they would not award a Pulitzer cartoon award that year because the year's cartoons didn't meet their lofty standards!

**HK:** If you were going to set up a board to review your work, what kind of people would be on that board, and what would you look for in a winning cartoon?

**PO:** Well, in this business I feel you're as good as you were yesterday. You get reviewed every day. I don't see the point in awards. With those things, when it's your turn, you'll get it. And some strange cartoons have received the Pulitzer Prize—mine being an example of it. I want to reject this whole thing. I was going to burn this drawing but I thought I'd better keep it and give it to the Library of Congress. You can have it.

**HK:** We're very grateful.

**PO:** So don't show it to anybody. Please. Or, if you must, please tell the whole story.

**HK:** Clearly the Pulitzer has been a very mixed result for you, but what prizes can do is at least represent some critical attention toward the work. Do you get that critical attention? Are there other sources you might trust?

**PO:** Just yourself, I think. Give myself an award. Or not. You're not trying to please an audience. If people like it, then that's good. I edit myself, because I work alone in the studio. I'm not reviewed. I suppose, if there was something really egregious, and I went crazy and did something that was uncharacteristic, my syndicate probably wouldn't send it out. But that's never happened to me. The syndicate likes me to express myself without restriction, and they take the brunt of any criticisms stoutly and without fear. I try to help defend them when I can. When I used to get mail, when people knew where to write to me, they would often reinforce my own idea of one of the main purposes of the cartoonist's role—as an articulator of ideas for people who don't have the opportunity to do that. In that sense, cartooning is a great privilege, being able to express something for people who either haven't thought of it that way, or seen that certain way of saying it.

**HK:** Well, you were at the *Denver Post* for, what, eleven or twelve years?

**PO:** Eleven years, and then I got a call one afternoon from Jim Bellows, who had just been

**[Destitute S&L please help]**

January 13, 1989
Ink and white out on paper,
11½ x 17 1/16 in.

On January 10, 1989, House Banking Committee members had their first look at details of the thirty-four thrift transactions arranged by the Federal Home Loan Bank Board (FHLBB) during December 1988. Tax breaks, totaling $8 billion during 1988, were guaranteed to buyers of insolvent institutions, much of it in the form of Federal Savings and Loan Insurance Corporation (FSLIC) notes. House members believed that the FHLBB had engaged in a gigantic giveaway of federal funds that benefited buyers, who invested little capital in return.

appointed editor of the Washington *[Evening] Star*, which had just recently been bought by Joe L. Albritton. And so he made me an offer I couldn't refuse, and I joined the Washington *Star* and looked out the window there on the first morning, and had much the same feeling I had had on that first morning at the *Denver Post* all those years before. What in the hell am I doing here? The *Star* was down in southeast D.C., amongst the projects, and next to a freeway, and didn't have much to do with Washington at all. It was in a hulking cinderblock building which I was told had won an award of some kind sometime in the '60s. It was one of those buildings they sold by the yard. How many floors of this one would you like? It was mostly lit by fluorescent light and the inside walls were tiled halfway up, so that the effect was of an enormous public toilet. We had to be escorted to and from our cars every day, and it was—it was not what you'd call a prime move, as far as I was concerned. Except that I was doing something different. I was working with the underdog, which was the Washington *Star* against the *Post*, which every chance it got would refer to us as the "financiallytroubled*Star*." One word. And we struggled on with that for six years, until 1981, when Time Incorporated bought the place, and they, having no idea how to run a newspaper, folded it in '81, and I've been in Washington ever since, trying to get out!

**HK:** What about your experience with the editor there at the *Star*?

**PO:** Oh, it was just completely open, so open I had no problem at all. We got along well, became friends, and we were working to stir things up. Trying to stir up the animals, as he called it, and . . . .

**HK:** Well, you were pretty much in agreement . . . .

**PO:** Yeah. He just wanted to stir things up. He really wanted to get a momentum going, and get attention to the newspaper to show that, after all these years as a conservative news-paper, it would now be a feisty contender. And he brought in all sorts of good names as writers in residence. He brought in Lawrence King, he brought in Willie Morris, Jimmy Breslin, George Higgins, and a lot of other people of that caliber. And so it was immense fun to be in such a situation for that length of time. We had a lot of excellent people putting out an excellent newspaper. But it just didn't have the local support. Newspapers were starting to go under. Afternoon newspapers were starting to fold up and die, because there was just not the readership and advertising support for them.

**HK:** For a while there, was it different from Denver? It sounds like you had more support in Washington.

REMEMBER TIANANMEN SQUARE

'HOLD IT...WAIT FOR ME!'

**PO:** I did. I had more interest taken in what I was doing. I felt more a part of it. That's probably why I made the change, because I felt it was time to do that. And it worked out wonderfully, except that the paper died.

**HK:** When the Washington *Star* folded, did you try to go to another newspaper, or did you decide deliberately to go on your own?

**PO:** I thought about it, and then I thought, here's a chance. I had always wanted to be independent. I had recently signed with Universal Press Syndicate, which is the best in the business. OK, I'll see if it works. So I've been on my own for sixteen years now. And I don't know if I could work for anybody anymore. It would be interesting, though, to be able to get the constant daily reaction. But I'd have to work with somebody who was willing to take the chance to stir things up, and I don't see that happening anywhere today for the very reasons we talked about. But who knows? I may end up with a paper again, because at least it's an outlet. At least it's a forum.

**HK:** Let's address the issue of independence. It's something that I know you feel strongly about, and I sort of like to bring up the example of Clifford Berryman, who was a Washington institution. He had a very good relationship with a lot of politicians and is considered one of the great American cartoonists.

**PO:** Some say.

**HK:** Some say. But what's wrong with that scenario?

**PO:** Being hand in glove with your subjects. I don't think that's good. Now, David Low used to do it and maintain a point of view. But I just wonder how independent I could stay, if I was doing a Berryman act. Probably not. And I don't think Berryman did. Well, he obviously didn't. And that is going to impact the work. But he didn't do anything really hard hitting, as far as a cartoon is concerned. He just drew their faces and stuck bodies on them. They were almost photographic faces. He didn't explore anything. So Berryman's not my . . . .

**HK:** What are you exploring? What are you looking for?

**PO:** With drawing, I'm looking for the unusual presentation, some twist that I haven't used before which will best convey what I'm trying to say. And I try to put a twist on what I'm trying to say too. Take it to the next stage each time. And when I've thought of an obvious cartoon, then don't be satisfied with that, but take it to the next stage, and then maybe a stage further, and see if you can see what sort of idea develops from that.

**'Hold it . . . wait for me!'**

August 23, 1989
Ink, brush and white out over pencil on layered paper, 11 11/16 x 17 1/2 in.

On August 19, 1989, more than 900 East German refugees in Hungary fled across the Hungarian border into Austria at the border town of Sopron, where a joint Hungarian-Austrian friendship picnic was taking place. Scores of East Germans had gathered in Sopron in anticipation of the opportunity to escape. When Hungarian border guards opened a frontier gate to let the Austrian picknickers through, about 300 East Germans rushed through into Austria. No effort was made to stop them and the guards left the gate open for hundreds of other East Germans to follow. This was believed to be the largest single illegal flight of East Germans to the West up to that point, and the Western press dubbed the incident the 'Great Escape.' The escapees began arriving in West Germany from Austria on August 21.

**HK:** Well, talking about independence, you've already said you need to remain apart from your subjects and not socialize with them. You've spoken of finding out that you actually liked Barry Goldwater.

**PO:** Sure. He's such an easy person to like. He believes in things. Whatever he said, he believed. You can get yourself awfully confused if you hang out with politicians. Your objectivity can suffer greatly. I just don't see any point in getting into that. Therefore, I can do my cartoons wherever I like. I'm not dependent on this town.

**HK:** You say you can live anywhere, but you do live in Washington. You do live close to where all the politicians live.

**PO:** Well, I joined the Washington *Star* in 1975, and it went belly up in '81, and I've been here ever since. I'm shipwrecked. I've been trying to get off this island for a long time. But at least it's close to New York.

**HK:** After the *Star* went under, you stayed with the syndicate, declining to join a newspaper. Do you miss working for a particular newspaper?

**PO:** I think there's a downside to it. This independence is good and great and lovely. And with today's technology, I can work anywhere. There are two things on the down side. One is that you're running your own business, buying your own materials, your own health insurance, there are no sweetheart deals. The other one is the lack of a daily reaction. It may get a bit better because, in syndication, we're now sending the cartoons out electronically. I scan them from my desk, and they go straight to my syndicate, and my syndicate scans them again and sends them out to the newspapers. And so they're used the next day in a lot of newspapers now. So it could be said that I've got lots of daily newspapers. If it were not for the fact that editors have become so timorous in these politically correct times, I would probably have a greater readership than I have. I expect we all would. But what we have in this country now is more and more one-newspaper towns. One-newspaper towns are not good because all the surviving newspaper does is print money. It's not printing newspapers at all, it's not serving the public. They make 25 percent on their money every year, and if they go down to 22 percent, then they start laying people off. So this is the sort of background we're drawing against.

**HK:** You mean the newspapers carry the ads and the classifieds, so they don't want to offend their advertisers?

**PO:** So now you've got that. Hey, nobody stir it up! Advertisers are uncomfortable with

"TIS THE SEASON TO BE JOLLY, MY GOOD MAN! WE WON – DID YOU KNOW THAT? CAPITALISM IS TRIUMPHANT. COMMUNISM LIES IN RUINS. OUR SYSTEM PREVAILS! WE WON! SMILE!'

controversy and their discomfort will show up on the paper's balance sheet, and affect the bottom line. The editors are themselves only too willing to do the bidding of these avaricious publishers. And these are the editors who were going to save us all. They were, most of them, in college in those days, during the Vietnam War. And this was the crowd that was in the streets, that we, as cartoonists, went about with. This was the tie-dyed generation in beards, beads, and bell bottoms that was going to save us all, who were so concerned about the beleaguered North Vietnamese that they were out burning the place and getting attention to the war. And Nixon, in his cunning, suddenly took away the draft, and they disappeared overnight. The cartoonists felt betrayed, because we were out there saying, "the war is still no damned good, where are you?" They'd gone back to college. The draft was gone and their asses were no longer on the line. And these people are now the editors. They've got 2.7 kids and 1.5 dogs and a mortgage, and they're just as hung up on all the material things as the people they disparaged in the '60s. So the race of editors that was supposed to come along and save us all, didn't. Now we've got an atmosphere where, ultimately, controversy is anathema. Which brings us into the politically correct arena.

**HK:** Do you think this is making a new generation of potential cartoonists think twice about creating controversy?

**PO:** I think so. Well, what they do is they just go for the gag now. They don't try to hit very hard. They can't hit very hard. They have editors to please. And so, where are we? We're back in the '50s. It's full circle. We've bred ourselves out. I sometimes feel really pessimistic about the future of good political cartooning.

**HK:** Now it seems as if special interest groups wield a great deal of power.

**PO:** That's right. I chafe about it all the time, because this is why I'm getting edited out. My audience isn't as big as it could be because of these timorous editors and the greedy publishers, and the flabby state of newspapers in general. And I wonder about the future of the business if this keeps up, and, ultimately, what is the point of it? Maybe we've seen our best days.

**HK:** I think the issue for a lot of people is that stereotyping—apart from whatever political message you were trying to put across—that the very presence of a negative stereotype, or a stereotype of any kind, is demeaning. And there's a sense, I think, among people who are complaining, that your work, and other work like it, is negative and insensitive, right from the start.

Isn't there a point at which your caricature of, say, Alan Greenspan could be mistaken

**[Fidel Castro building a sand castle]**

January 10, 1990
Ink and white out over pencil on layered paper, 11⅝ x 17⁹⁄₁₆ in.

The member states of the Council for Mutual Economic Assistance (Comecon), the Soviet-bloc trade organization, agreed on January 10, 1990, at the conclusion of a heated two-day summit in Sofia, Bulgaria, to adopt a gradual free-market approach in their trading policies. Cuba, Vietnam, and Mongolia, the non-European members, were not enthusiastic about the proposed changes. They indicated that their economies would continue along traditional Marxist lines, no matter what policies Comecon adopted.

# The Persian Gulf War

'HOW COZY IT IS ON THESE COLD WINTER EVENINGS, TO SNUGGLE DOWN IN FRONT OF TV AND WATCH THE WAR.'

**'How cozy it is on these cold winter evenings, to snuggle down in front of TV and watch the war.'**

January 22, 1991
Ink and white out over pencil on paper,
11⁹⁄₁₆ x 17¹⁄₁₆ in.

An international force led by the U.S. launched an air missile attack against Iraq and Iraqi-occupied Kuwait on January 16, 1991, after Iraq failed to withdraw its troops from Kuwait. Iraqi President Saddam Hussein announced the next day that "the mother of all battles" had begun. Code-named "Operation Desert Storm," the Persian Gulf War involved the use of high-technology weaponry, with strikes launched from bases in Saudi Arabia and Bahrain and from ships in the region. The Department of Defense exercised complete control over press coverage during the first month of the war, convinced that the grisly pictures that came out of Vietnam had swung public opinion against that war. Various U.S. media outlets complained that the system did not permit free flow of news, and that the daily allied military briefings in Riyadh, the Saudi capital, presented a manipulated, sanitized account of the war.

## 'Oo! Is it too late to go back to sanctions?'

February 14, 1991
Ink and white out over pencil on paper,
11⁹⁄₁₆ x 17 in.

On February 13, scores of Iraqi civilians were killed when U.S. bombs destroyed a reinforced building where they had taken refuge from the nightly bombing. Television pictures from Baghdad showed badly burned survivors of the attack, shocking and angering many members of the public.

as a general statement against Jews in power, one of your cartoons on ebonics considered a racial slur, or a satire on papal policy as a personal attack on the Pope?

**PO:** I draw Greenspan as I see him. I mean, it's a set of features. He has a rather large nose. Good. Here we have physiognomy I can really get into. If he was an Arab, and incidentally also a Semite, there would be no problem. No one would complain, because they've got no lobby. I draw Al Sharpton—how am I supposed to draw him? Looking like Superman? I mean, these are people who just have an appearance which lends itself to caricature, and you're not going after their personal beliefs, or their race, or their ethnic origins.

**HK:** What role does the stereotype play? What does it do for you?

**PO:** Well, in an art of symbols, it helps. It helps me depict a person recognizably. We're always up against people not being recognized. I hate it when there's a change of adminis-trations because there's a whole new cast of characters coming along which must be seen in newspapers and on television for about six months before your caricatures become recognized, simply because your audience has to become used to the faces of the new line-up. And so when you've got a set of features like Greenspan's, which are wonderfully recognizable features, what do I soften? I mean, what on earth can I soften? Here is the quintessential accountant. A *Victorian* accountant. A *Dickensian* accountant, f'God's sake. It's too delicious to refuse.

**HK:** Do you sometimes regret that maybe a point of your message may be lost because somebody is going to respond negatively to what they see?

**PO:** You have to be careful of that. But you have to stick with it. I mean, Herblock really earned his stripes back in the '50s in the McCarthy era. He stuck to what he believed, right through that thing. He was more than instrumental in bringing down McCarthy. I mean, he really had a big part in it. And he's the only cartoonist I know who's had a whole newspaper built around him, because of that. There were dragons to slay in those days. And there hasn't been anything like that since, except for Nixon. Nixon was a good dragon.

**HK:** What about the issue of whether you're trying to provoke a response, or persuade?

**PO:** Well, I think the cartoon should start some sort of dialogue in the letters column. One should be provoking and provocative. I've never been able to determine whether a cartoon can ever persuade, that is, actually change somebody's mind. I think that, if it happens at all, the work is probably done through presenting the prickly aspects of a controversy or promoting a dia-logue. From that may come some good. Putting the cat amongst the pigeons, I think it's called.

**[Jesse Helms attacks cultural funding]**

March 6, 1992
Ink and white out over pencil on layered paper, 11½ x 17½ in.

During the 1992 presidential campaign, conservative Republicans led by Senator Jesse Helms targeted federal funding for the National Endowment for the Arts (NEA) and the Public Broadcasting Service (PBS). Pat Buchanan, another con-servative who was challenging President George Bush for the Republican presidential nomination, chastised Bush for allowing the NEA to fund "pornographic art" and called the endowment "the uphol-stered playpen of the arts and crafts auxiliary of the Eastern liberal establishment." The White House forced John Frohnmayer, chairman of the NEA, to resign on February 29. Republican members of Congress attempted to eliminate these programs from the federal budget in 1992.

**HK:** Has the power of the special interests sort of overwhelmed our national sense of identity? Have we lost our sense of humor as a nation?

**PO:** Actually, in a country so charged with all the elements of the hilarious, the preposterous, the wildly ridiculous, it is hard to imagine this could happen. But I think we have, or at least we are working on it. You don't hear people telling jokes any more. It might offend some-body, I guess. There used to be, not so long ago, a great undercurrent of funny stuff going around, but not even the Clintons have spawned much of a school of jokes. And they should, if anybody does.

**HK:** Let's talk about humor. Because you know, from my perspective, a lot of people talk about cartoons in general and think of humor as a vehicle for carrying a message. But you seem to differentiate between a gag and what you're doing. Talk a little bit more about that.

**PO:** Humor is, of course, like you said, a great vehicle for getting a serious message across. And, in fact, it maybe sugarcoats the pill . . . you can be serious and humorous at the same time. Better than being just blindly savage about something. But we're not allowed to joke very much these days. What has occurred? What *was* that—the rise of feminism? Notoriously humorless. And there's a huge surge of religiosity in this country as part of the movement not to offend anybody. When you get these special interests intimidating the advertisers who intimidate the publishers who intimidate the editors, it can certainly take the edge off cartooning of the more challenging type.

**HK:** Where do you draw the line about what to include in your cartoons?

**PO:** Oh, making fun of the helpless. Most people aren't helpless, though. So most people are as fair game as any politician. But, as cartoonists, we're supposed to be small "l" liberal and for the underdog. So we're not likely to launch our day by mocking the halt, the lame, the helpless, or the disadvantaged.

**HK:** How many of your colleagues achieve that kind of high-mindedness, and how well do you achieve it?

**PO:** Well, you'll see some cartoonists who want to draw people without any racial characteris-tics at all. Blacks look like whites, like Hispanics, like Arabs, you know. They all look correctly caucasian, so that nobody is going to be stirred up. Ridiculous. As I say, the whole spice of life comes from the differentiation. I drew George Wallace in a wheelchair once. Got all sorts of crap for that. He was in a wheelchair at the time. It was after the attempted assassination.

THEN, WE HAVE TO TRY TO GET WHATEVER IS LEFT, ELECTED.

THE DEMOCRATIC FIELD AT THIS TIME.

**HK:** How do you fight that kind of criticism?

**PO:** I come armed with experience. It's the same people who were telling me what cartoons to draw on those afternoons in Adelaide in the 1950s. Cartoon by committee. Or, more accurately, blacksmithing by committee.

**HK:** Only at least, now, you're in a position where you can do what you want.

**PO:** I can at least ignore them.

**HK:** You really miss the atmosphere of the '60s and '70s, don't you?

**PO:** Newspaper cartoons still had some strength as forums for ideas then. I think it was the last period when we could just rely on the medium to carry it. I think most of the editorial boards were behind us at that time, against the war. That quickening feeling of everything being united for this common cause, get rid of this damn war, nobody wants it. And that was a uniting feeling. On the other hand, I think we were fairly competitive about who could do the best job of getting the message across. But the '60s and '70s sort of cheapened the language somewhere. It used to be fun to cuss, swearing was fun. Still is a handy emphasis, but somewhere along the way, the kids, the hippie generation, to be more precise, devalued the currency. Now it seems you can use any word you want publicly, it will appear anywhere you look—T-shirts to bumper stickers. The powers of subtlety have been weakened by the fact that you can say anything. Condom cartoons, for instance, would never have been done in those days. This does not, of course, mean that one must stand rooted in the past. But so much of what was provocative has been cheapened, taken away, or deadened by overuse. The currency has been devalued. So that's another weakening of this business.

**HK:** Has it made you go into areas that you wouldn't have looked at before? Are there positive ways that you've found to provoke, or get under somebody's skin?

**PO:** No. I'm trying the same things I always did, because I think they still work. I've tried to keep in mind what was valuable to me when I started in this business, which is, I hope, subtlety. Humor, and subtlety in humor, are still valuable, and I still want to use them that way, and I think they're still valid and effective, despite my aforesaid lament. And, although I enjoy the words, I won't allow myself to use them in cartoons, because, hopefully, it's still a family newspaper. The restrictions which I just railed about I am now supporting in some strange way—talk about contradictions.

**[Free at last!]**

April 30, 1992
Ink and white out over pencil on paper,
11½ x 17 in.

Oliphant used the Reverend Martin Luther King, Jr.'s famous words from the civil rights era to underscore, with great irony, what he believed to be a travesty of justice, the jury acquittal on April 29, 1992, of four white Los Angeles police officers accused of beating black motorist Rodney G. King in March 1991. In the wake of riots that ensued in the South-Central district of Los Angeles, in which fifty-eight people were killed and $1 billion of damage was done, President George Bush said, "The jury system has worked. What's needed now is calm, respect for the law." The riots focused the country's attention on continuing inequities and tension between blacks and whites in the United States.

**HK:** What about differences in your source material? Are there traditional source materials, such as literary, historical, or art-historical allusions, that you can no longer turn to in creating your cartoons because your average reader can't understand them?

**PO:** Well, you just about answered your own question right there. People are reading less. The sources of learning, which used to teach handy skills like reading, I recently heard described as "our Playschool education system." Don't you love terms like that? Twenty short years ago I could use a Hamlet or Macbeth analogy in a cartoon and it would be understood as a matter of course. I could refer to Twain, or Defoe, or Edgar Allan Poe. Nevermore. The background is not taught, therefore there is no context or point of reference for those educated in this country in the past twenty years, which would enable them to understand what the hell I'm talking about. My art is, therefore, diminished in direct proportion to the ignorance of the viewer. Probably it could be written as a mathematical theorem—cartooning divided by ignorance squared equals zero. Class dismissed.

**HK:** So that kind of blandness has its counterpart in the political realm.

**PO:** Yeah. It almost makes you *like* Jesse Helms. He at least believes in something. You may hate him, but, damn it, I think if all Democrats were like Clinton, I'd be a Republican. And if all Republicans were like McCain of Arizona, I'd certainly be a Republican. I like him, you know. I'd better be damn sure not ever to meet him.

**HK:** What did Nixon mean to your career?

**PO:** He meant a great deal, I think. Meant a great deal to quite a few people, cartoonists especially, in that he polarized everybody. Everybody was after him, and I tried to do a better job than anybody else.

**HK:** What about his features? I mean, what kind of elements went into your cartoons?

**PO:** Well, he had sort of a dark history. He was already established as a caricature. You didn't have to do the obligatory six months to establish him. He wrote his own stuff, you know. As Mark Russell would call it, rip and read. You just took it off the printer and read it, and it was a cartoon. Believe it or not, you had to concentrate very hard to keep a handle on the whole era, because there was so much juicy, diverting stuff going on. You had to see where it was going, so you could have a continuum to your work. But it was easy to get sidetracked in an entertaining carnival such as this was.

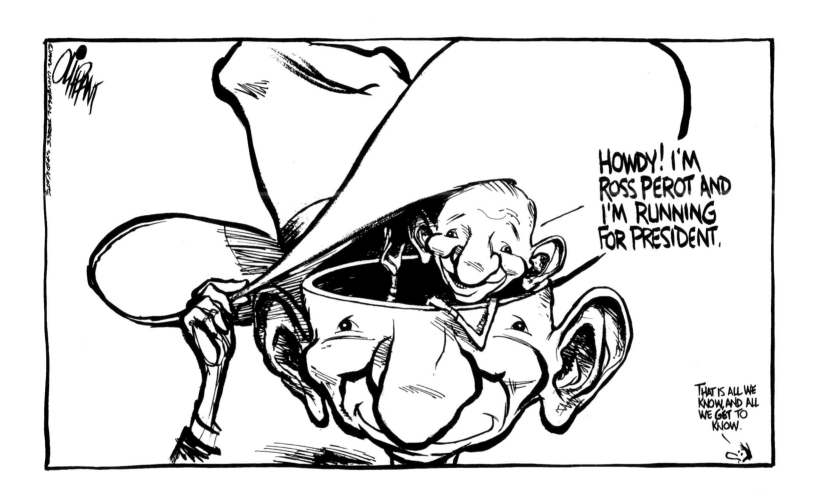

'EITHER ALL OUR CHICKENS CAME HOME TO ROOST, OR THIS IS THE ARKANSAS TRANSITION TEAM.'

**'Either all our chickens came home to roost, or this is the Arkansas transition team.'**

November 6, 1992
Ink and white out over pencil on paper,
11⅝ x 17 in.

Arkansas Governor Bill Clinton was elected the forty-second president of the United States on November 3, 1992. During the final days of the campaign President George Bush asserted that Clinton and Gore were untested leaders; "My dog Millie knows more about foreign policy than these two bozos," he said during his visit to Michigan. During the campaign, Clinton had been derided by Republicans for the limitations of his experience as the governor of a rural, sparsely populated state, whose economy relied heavily on chicken farming.

MORNING AGAIN??

IT'S REVEILLE IN AMERICA!

### It's reveille in America!

February 18, 1993
Ink and white out over pencil on paper,
11½ x 16¹⁵⁄₁₆ in.

President Bill Clinton presented his economic program on February 17, 1993, in a nationally televised address to a joint session of Congress. The proposal included tax increases and the most ambitious deficit reduction plan since World War II. Clinton's call for fiscal reform was widely seen as shaping the entire legislative agenda for his term and as a dramatic reversal of the fiscal policies of the Reagan-Bush presidencies. Republicans were quick to criticize the tax hikes and congressional support for the plan appeared unsteady, even among Democrats. Clinton had been featured playing his saxophone on numerous occasions throughout the campaign and at the inaugural festivities.

**HK:** The Watergate hearings were must-see stuff.

**PO:** Yeah, it was all a major cartoon. I wonder, if it happened today, whether the reactions to the cartoons would be the same, because people are getting all their news from television, not reading newspapers much. Would we have had the same influence, or got the same reactions, today as we did then? Maybe not. People aren't reading. They're just getting it all off the tube. And yet TV won't function as a forum for cartoons because TV is scared of the controversy it might stir up. I don't think we'll ever get on the screen in that way, although I do believe that cartooning would be wonderfully served by letting people *see* it drawn, right in front of them, on the screen. And I like to do that. When I give talks, I have a TV camera up there above my head and drawing board, and then a couple of big TV screens on the side. And you can hold an audience for hours, so long as you keep drawing. They just love to watch it happen. It's like looking over somebody's shoulder while they're sketching. And that would be the natural way to do it on television. But the TV people are scared of the art, anyway. They don't want it to happen because by its very nature it's controversial. So newspapers and TV are now very much the same and there's really nowhere to go. Which is bad news, both for up-and-coming cartoonists and for the art itself. How can it survive if it's not being nurtured by new talent?

**HK:** Well, we had Nixon in the '60s, and now we've got Clinton in the '90s. You've answered the question of whether it was a rich period for your profession then, but what about now? It seems like there is a lot of material, a lot of scandal. But what's different?

**PO:** Clinton has committed the greatest sin a politician can commit. He's boring. I can't feign any interest in drawing him. Even his scandals are boring to me. There's no jokes going on about him. Nobody seems to care much about Clinton. If ever there was a Teflon president, it's Clinton, not Reagan.

**HK:** Can you compare those two administrations, Clinton and Reagan, what Reagan meant to you?

**PO:** Oh, Reagan. You know, I tried to fan a dislike of Reagan. Nobody would have it, and it was hard work for eight years, trying to convince an audience that a lot of these policies had holes in them. And you couldn't help but like him, grudgingly. You compare him with Clinton, you kind of like him a bit. At least in his own way. A, he was fun to draw, and B, he at least believed in something, whatever it was. This guy we've got right now—there's nothing to grab onto. It's like fighting with cotton candy. There's not much there. And God forbid that we

---

**Nine lives and counting . . .**

March 25, 1993
Ink and white out over pencil on paper,
11½ x 17⅟₁₆ in.

Russian leader Boris Yeltsin engaged in a power struggle for control of the country with his parliamentary opponents in the Supreme Soviet, leading him to claim special emergency powers in a televised address on March 20, 1993. This followed a week in which the Congress of People's Deputies, led by chairman Ruslan I. Khasbulatov, voted to take away prerogatives granted to Yeltsin in December 1992. Yeltsin modified his decree when it was published on March 24 and did not mention "special powers." The Constitutional Court, which convened on March 22, ruled that Yeltsin's actions had violated provisions of the constitution. The Court argued that Yeltsin did not have the right to ask the populace to choose between presidential or parliamentary control of the government. Khasbulatov called for Yeltsin's impeachment.

NINE LIVES AND COUNTING...

'THANK YOU FOR NOT INTERFERING.'

have to draw Gore for four or eight years. That would be hell. That's why I voted for Reagan once, because he was running against Mondale. I didn't want to draw Mondale for four years. But I was voting in the District of Columbia so it was a pretend-vote anyway.

**HK:** What about George Bush and his handbag?

**PO:** Well, I find myself doing that with cartoons. This is an art of symbols, and the symbols aren't always obvious in these rather dull days at the end of the twentieth century, where every politician looks the same, they all dress the same, and they talk the same. You have to invent symbols for yourself. Like the purse for Bush. It was born of a reaction. He took his glasses off when he was campaigning the first time because he felt they made him look like a wimp. So for all the rest of us who wear glasses, I always drew him wearing glasses from that point on. And I added the purse as punitive damages.

**HK:** So we've discussed a little bit the tough shape that the profession is in, with dwindling newspapers, dwindling markets, political correctness, all the things that really make it difficult for editorial cartoonists these days. What keeps you motivated and keeps you coming back?

**PO:** Oh, I think it's a compulsion. After forty years of doing it, I love to do it. I think I know how to do it now. Especially when it all keeps coming back.

**HK:** The material keeps coming back?

**PO:** Yeah. That doesn't mean that I've got my idea all set for the day, because it's difficult. I mean, you get up in the morning. You don't know what's going to hit you, or not hit you. You're never sure—because things can change overnight—what you're going to be doing in the morning. Which A, may make life interesting, or B, may make it miserable. But I take the attitude that the glass is half full and I'll be able to handle this tomorrow. But it's always a surprise. I'll think in my head that I have a great idea—terrific—and I'll think on it all night, on the rare occasions when I do that, and then I'll draw it in the morning . . . and it doesn't work at all. So then I've got to start work all over again, rethinking the thing. And when you do that, reworking an idea, you'll most times find it doesn't work, and you've got to go on to another subject. But whatever it is, I've got to have some feeling about it, I've got to be exercised about it to some degree.

**HK:** Do you think that kind of passion is necessary to an editorial?

**PO:** Yes.

**HK:** Is it important to have a viewpoint going in that you adhere to?

**PO:** Sometimes, when you go in, you don't know what your viewpoint is. You work that out as you go along. And you sometimes will come up with a cartoon which is a great idea and would make a wonderful drawing but, unfortunately, it's an idea totally contrary to the point of view you've come to believe should be expressed. So you scrap it and start over.

**HK:** What's consistent? What's going to be the same in an Oliphant cartoon from day to day?

**PO:** A general feeling of fair play, I hope. A feeling of distrust for lawyers, politicians, and the running dogs of that ilk. Just the dislike of banality and greed, and those people who are in a position to do good and instead do the opposite.

**HK:** Do you feel it's a homogenized time we're in?

**PO:** Yeah. There are not enough differences to grab onto, are there? But now corporations are treating employees in the manner of the old Robber Barons. And organized labor is coming back. And the cycle is starting again.

**HK:** Well, you seem, on the one hand, to support the working man and, on the other hand, to attack the unions.

**PO:** Yeah. There's a difference, you know. I just play that issue by issue. I think that pretty much sums up what the charter of the cartoonist is, at least the liberal cartoonist. Or the *skeptical* liberal cartoonist. Liberalism—small "l"—being synonymous with a good democracy. And I just like what this country stands for. That's why I'm here. That's why you're here, you know. It's a good place to be. It's the great experiment. It's still the great experiment. May it always be.

**HK:** Right. Let's shift gears and talk about how your art has evolved over the years. We're looking now at a group of drawings from the '60s and '70s. Tell me about the materials and methods you used earlier in your career.

**PO:** I think all of these cartoons we are looking at are drawn on a prepared paper called duoshade, which is preprinted with a chemical which, when painted with a special developer, brings up a diagonal line tone and then, when it's treated with another developer, will bring out a cross-hatch. And I used this in Australia because, before that, to get the effect of a third tone, we would be forced to stick down a plastic sheet printed with tonal dots, called Ben-Day, that you put down over the drawing and then went over with an Exacto knife and hauled out the bits that you didn't want. This could take hours. So when we found there was

a paper that actually would do that, it became very popular. I can't say it was a great gift because, archivally, it's a terrible paper. The drawings tend to be fugitive in areas where the chemical was used, although the inkwork remains stable. You can see, with quite a few of these drawings, how the stuff, even if it is stored in the dark, will decay, become brown, and, in some cases, disappear altogether. And so it was strictly for reproduction. But it was not for building a body of work.

**HK:** When did you decide to take another look at your working practices?

**PO:** Around 1980 I experienced a renaissance of sorts. I looked at my drawing and I wasn't pleased with it. I didn't like the way it was going, I didn't like this paper, I thought I should be getting more into my drawing than I was getting, acknowledging that when you cartoon it's easy to get into bad habits. Then you tend to start drawing by code and you'll just get sloppy unless you review what you're doing every so often and go back over a year's work and say, well, this was better than that, I should have kept this, I should throw that out, how can I improve this, and so forth. So I went through one of those periods of reassessment.

**HK:** During the '60s and '70s, you were just moving ahead?

**PO:** Moving ahead, headlong, and not paying too much attention, or enough attention, to what we are talking about. I find that drawing is an ongoing study. If you're an artist, it's a thing you devote yourself to for the rest of your life and you're always learning something, always changing. Or you should be always changing. I find that I'll work in a certain manner for a while and then I'll reassess myself and then go start something else. So that's the fun of it, really. There are voyages of self-discovery to find out what you can do and what you've forgotten to do, and surprising yourself all the time with different things.

**HK:** Were there any reassessments earlier in your career?

**PO:** I think so, yeah. But I think that, up until that time in the '80s, I was not paying enough attention to the other things I could have been doing, or should have been doing.

**HK:** Artistically?

**PO:** Artistically, being painting, for one thing, and drawing from life, something which is tremendously important, I think.

**HK:** These are things that you had done in your youth but you had let go for a couple of decades?

**[Rabin, Arafat, and dove of peace]**

September 14, 1993
Ink and white out over pencil on paper, 11⁹⁄₁₆ x 17¹⁄₁₆ in.

Yitzhak Rabin, the prime minister of Israel, and Yasir Arafat, the chairman of the Palestine Liberation Organization (PLO) shook hands on the White House lawn on September 13, 1993, sealing an accord that committed Israelis and Palestinians to share a land they both claimed as their own. Minutes earlier, Israeli Foreign Minister Shimon Peres and the PLO's chief negotiator with Israel, Mahmoud Abbas, signed a declaration of principles for interim Palestinian self-government in the Gaza Strip and the West Bank town of Jericho.

**'Now, tell the jury what
you did with the knife,
Mrs. Bobbitt...'**

January 12, 1994
Ink and white out over pencil on paper,
11⁷⁄₁₆ x 16¹⁵⁄₁₆ in.

The trial of twenty-four-year-old
Ecuadoran native Lorena Bobbit for
cutting off her husband's penis in
June 1993 ran through December
and January, ending with her acquittal
by reason of insanity on January 21,
1994. A jury in Manassas, Virginia, and
a rapt worldwide audience, listened
to the young woman's account of
sexual abuse by her husband, culmi-
nating in the alleged marital rape
which led her to retaliate. Reactions
to both the cutting and the verdict
were often split along gender lines
and spurred a national debate on
domestic violence. Some men's
groups argued that an acquittal of
Lorena Bobbit might encourage other
women to perform similar attacks
on men.

**PO:** Yeah, for a long time. And, you know, I thought it was about time to stage a renaissance here and see what I had been reflecting and what should I be getting out of it. So, later into the '80s, around '84, '85, I was asked to address a class at the Corcoran School by a teacher who is a friend of mine, Bill Christenberry, and I liked the feeling of things. It reminded me so strongly of what I hadn't been doing that I enrolled with Bill's group there, drawing from the model, and worked at it twice weekly for two or three years. It was a wonderful thing to do, to go back to drawing from the actual human form.

**HK:** So you were drawing from a model in those classes?

**PO:** Yeah, a model. And, of course, there's nothing wrong with going a couple of times a week to look at a naked lady. Christenberry still laughs about this: I would get to the door and, if it was a male model, I'd go home. I told him if I wanted to draw a naked man I could look in the mirror! He still tells that story, and, believe me, it loses nothing in the telling!

**HK:** Well, do you see yourself as an artist or as a cartoonist?

**PO:** I try to see myself as an artist who happens to do cartoons. I want to bring that element to it.

**HK:** How is the art acting on your drawings?

**PO:** First, I like what it does to your mind, the way it frees you up when you're working from one thing to another. You go from having a painting going in one room and then back to the cartoon. It can happen with sculpture, too, but that's messier. It's not that it will echo immediately in the drawing that you're working on, because that has its own place to go. It's what it does to your thinking and how it disengages you from it temporarily, so that you can come back fresh to it.

**HK:** Are you a doodler?

**PO:** Oh, yeah. I've always been a doodler. It's a funny thing, the most strange and creative things come out of doodling when you're on the phone and one part of your mind is turned off and you start drawing. I think that's the path to true abstraction, if you can teach yourself to turn off one part of your mind and switch to another.

**HK:** Do the doodles ever turn into something you can use?

**PO:** They have in later years. These things tend to accumulate on my drawing board. I have let them accumulate for a few years and then cut out the parts that interest me and work

'NOW, TELL THE JURY WHAT YOU DID WITH THE KNIFE, MRS. BOBBITT...'

back into them. They become in the process quite interesting abstracts. And of course that's another area altogether. Abstraction's one of the most difficult areas I've ever explored because, for the last forty or so years, I've approached a piece of blank paper with the need to have an idea and translate that idea into a drawing and present it that way. Whereas, with abstraction, you just let the paint do it, let the instruments do it, and you follow along down wondrous, serendipitous paths of discovery. It's a difficult thing to do, to learn to turn off that part of your mind and turn on another part. . . . I think it helps everything. And it's a respite. But, most importantly, it's a voyage of discovery that you wouldn't otherwise experience.

**HK:** Pat, when did you start working with sculpture, prints, and monotypes?

**PO:** In the early '80s, at the National Gallery of Art, I saw a huge retrospective of Rodin's work and I was amazed at the scope of his work with the figure. This inspired me to begin working in wax and I found myself suddenly in a world which seemed to open off in all directions, each promising and irresistible. Because I had always been captivated by Daumier's work, in particular his caricature sculptures of the French assembly, and because caricature was a natural gravitational point, I started work fashioning caricature likenesses of presidents, senators, and congressmen. From there, I moved to other subject matter, different people, animals, birds. About that time, I came to the realization that it is difficult for an artist known in one area to move into another. There is a tendency for observers to pigeonhole you into the mold previously set. You are known as a painter, you are, therefore, a painter. You are a cartoonist, you are, and shall ever remain, a cartoonist. And so on. It is immensely difficult to roll that rock out of the path. Not that that is deterring or impossible to overcome, far from it. But it is there, nonetheless.

Lithography I first explored at the Tamarind Institute in Albuquerque in 1976. Then, too, I stayed with what I knew, a caricature of Nelson Rockefeller as St. Francis of Assisi. I have done many lithographs since, but none in four colors, as that one was. Monotypes I discovered a few years back at the studio of a friend in Santa Fe. Two of these first attempts are in this show. I was so pleased with the results, it compelled me to get a press of my own. The main difference between lithographs and monotypes is that the former is a collaborative effort between the artist and the printer. The other is a solitary exercise, like drawing, but, in some strange way, is much less inhibiting and more spontaneous. And then, of course, lithography offers many prints from the same stone. The monotype, as its name suggests, is a unique impression.

**RMN. Lest we forget**

April 28, 1994
Ink and white out over pencil on layered paper, 11½ x 17 in.

Richard Milhous Nixon, 37th President of the United States, died April 22, 1994, from complications of a severe stroke. Nixon's career as a political figure and statesman spanned nearly five decades, including 20 years in which he held elective office as a congressman, senator, vice president, and president. His accomplishments were overshadowed by the legacy of the Watergate scandal. He was buried April 27, 1994, on the grounds of his birthplace in Yorba Linda, California, after a nationally televised funeral.

**HK:** During the '60s and '70s, I think you worked out your preliminary sketches on newsprint, is that right?

**PO:** Uh-huh.

**HK:** So what happened, when did you start working with sketchbooks?

**PO:** Probably when I went to the *Star*, I think I started using sketchbooks there. Or maybe when I started working at home. Newsprint was quick and easy, an always-at-hand sort of drawing material. Once again, we weren't looking to preserve anything.

**HK:** Right. So you're still thinking in terms of just creating these drawings for reproduction. What did the sketchbook do for you and how do you use it?

**PO:** Well, I enjoy seeing how the drawings develop. I enjoy being able to go back through the sketchbook—which is on acid-free paper, drawing in pencil—and just being able to see what I've done from years before.

**HK:** When you're going to draw a cartoon, do you sometimes go back to your sketchbooks to see if there are drawings you did before that didn't work out, that you might want to go back to and try again?

**PO:** I suppose, though I can't really drag out of my memory what I may have done that way. I will develop caricatures sometimes in a sketchbook, and they'll get swallowed up as the pages keep turning, and I'll go back and look at everything to see what I was doing. So I do a drawing in the sketchbook, which is the first realization of the idea, see if it works, then I go to a pencil drawing, and then I ink over that. That's the third stage. And I'm probably more pleased with drawings if I put the idea directly down with pen. Drawings that I've done that way always work out well, there's even more spontaneity to them. But I'm not brave enough to work that way on a daily basis.

**HK:** It seems to me as if this recent interest in varied art media, materials, and methods has enabled you to develop an expanded arsenal of styles. Do you change styles according to the content of the message?

**PO:** Yeah, I do. Looking at this drawing from 1989, "Remember Tiananmen Square" (page 47), the face and the figure are drawn starkly and fairly straight because you're dealing with a serious subject in a serious manner. You're not going to depict it with a drawing of what you would term a humorous stereotype. And there's no penguin. [The pencil drawing that appears on page 47 was added for this publication.]

'I'VE GOT AN IDEA FOR '96 — I GO BACK, I BEG FORGIVENESS, PLAY THE WHOLE REDEMPTION BIT,
THE REFORMED UNDERDOG BACK FROM HELL, I GET RE-ELECTED, WE TAKE OVER...'

# Sketchbooks

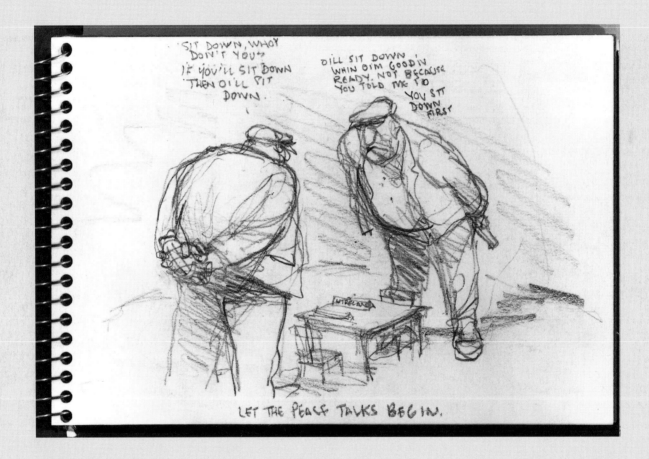

**Let the Peace Talks Begin,** 1993

Page from a sketchbook.
Pencil on paper, 4 x 6 in.

**Sit down, whoy don't you?
If you'll sit down, then oi'll
sit down, then we'll be all
sittin' down.**

September 2, 1994
Ink and white out over pencil on paper,
11⁹⁄₁₆ x 15¾ in.

In interviews on September 1, 1994, Gerry Adams, president of Sinn Fein, the political wing of the outlawed Provisional Irish Republican Army, and leading Sinn Fein strategist Martin McGuinness faulted the government of British Prime Minister John Major for refusing to enter into peace talks with them until three months after the truce announced by the Irish Republican Army on August 31. Peace talks between Irish Prime Minister Albert Reynolds and Gerry Adams finally began on September 6.

**Off to the Revolution,** 1994

Page from a sketchbook.
Pencil on paper, 4 x 6 in.

OFF TO THE REVOLUTION.

**Off to the revolution.**

January 6, 1995
Ink and white out over pencil on
paper, 11⁹⁄₁₆ x 15¹⁄₁₆ in.

The 104th Congress convened on January 4, 1995, with the Republican Party, under the leadership of new House Speaker Newt Gingrich and new Senate Majority Leader Robert J. Dole, holding majorities in both the House and the Senate for the first time in forty years. GOP lawmakers hailed the new term as a major step in the "Republican revolution" while formerly dominant Democrats struggled to adapt to minority status. In September 1994, more than three hundred GOP House candidates had signed a "Contract with America," a campaign manifesto drawn up by Gingrich that included such bill proposals as The Fiscal Responsibility Act, The Taking Back Our Streets Act, The Personal Responsibility Act, The Family Reinforcement Act, The American Dream Restoration Act, The National Security Restoration Act, The Senior Citizens Fairness Act, The Job Creation and Wage Enhancement Act, The Common Sense Legal Reform Act, and The Citizen Legislature Act.

**[Buchanan and his
Advisors],** 1996

Page from a sketchbook.
Pencil on paper, 4 x 6 in.

**Where the Elephants
Went to Die,** 1996

Page from a sketchbook.
Pencil on paper, 4 x 6 in.

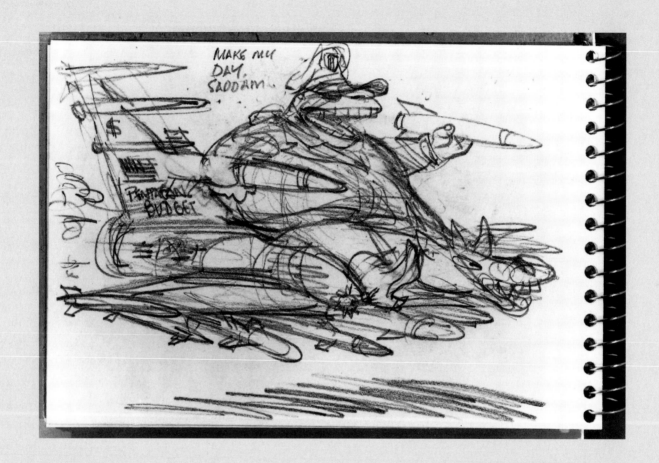

**Make My Day, Saddam,** 1996

Page from a sketchbook.
Pencil on paper, 4 x 6 in.

**[Clinton the Bobby and Kuwait],** 1996

Page from a sketchbook
Pencil on paper, 4 x 6 in.

**Four More Years of
Whomever [Clinton],** 1996

Page from a sketchbook.
Pencil on paper, 4 x 6 in.

**[Joe Camel],** 1997

Page from a sketchbook
Pencil on paper, 4 x 6 in.

**HK:** OK, this one deals with East Germany and the fall of Communism. It's really a wonderful drawing, called "Hold it, wait for me" (page 48), again from 1989. Both of these drawings have aspects that are very impressionistic.

**PO:** Cartoonists are indeed impressionists, you know. Those buildings there are put in quickly with a brush, and then the rest of it is done mostly with pen. But the background is put in quickly so you can see it as buildings without consciously bothering too much. It's just strokes of the brush to get the windows, to get a certain stark, skull-like effect into those buildings. So a cartoon is a sketch, it's an impressionist drawing or painting, whatever. You should be able to see color, if it's done properly.

**HK:** This one is called "Tis the season to be jolly, my good man!" (page 51), and again it's from 1989. It's the post-Cold War image of a capitalist talking to a homeless man.

**PO:** A certain amount of Scrooge to it. These figures are all in black suits, lumbering, successful capitalists.

**HK:** So, compare that with "Remember Tiananmen Square," and what you're trying to accomplish.

**PO:** There's a starkness to that, but this is different. I mean, it's a tragic thing, but it's drama in a different way. It wasn't as dramatically tragic. It's impressionistic in the background, done quickly with a brush just to give hurrying figures and a snowy Christmas evening. But there is a penguin in this one.

**HK:** So there are times when you don't feel it's appropriate to use Punk.

**PO:** You'll notice with certain serious cartoons like this one, or that wretched Pulitzer thing, I didn't put him in. I don't put him in that sort of cartoon because it would be too flip and flippant to do. For example, when you've got an assassination to deal with, you can't have some smart guy yapping from the side, you know. So, in those situations I leave him out. He understands.

**HK:** What about this S&L bailout drawing (page 44), another 1989 cartoon, in yet another style? Talk a little bit about how that might differ from "Tiananmen Square." This is a serial drawing....

**PO:** It's a serial drawing. It's got a simple figure which I use as sort of a symbol for Everyman or . . . .

'YOU MAY BE THE COMMANDING GENERAL OF POST 17 OF THE GRAND PATRIOT MILITIA, BUT IN THIS OUTFIT YOU'RE THE PRIVATE WHO TAKES THE GARBAGE TO THE DUMP!'

'I WAS ABOUT TO SAY THAT IF OL' J. EDGAR WAS STILL RUNNING THINGS, WE WOULDN'T BE HAVING THIS BIG IMAGE PROBLEM... BUT LET IT PASS.'

**HK:** John Q. Public.

**PO:** John Q. Public, as you call it. A built-in victim. And, of course, this was at the time when the S&Ls were being bailed out, whether we liked it or not, and this is what I saw was happening. This is whimsy—all drawn with a pen, all white lines and all fairly loose, a nice lot of action to it, starting static and ending static, with the four panels of things happening. Sometimes that serial way is the best way to tell a story. It's a narrative, it's a little story, it's a one-act play. And, in this case, it's pantomime.

**HK:** It seems like you've really developed a broad range of styles over the past fifteen years.

**PO:** It's a vocabulary. So many cartoonists draw the same year after year. When they find a style, they stick with it. They don't mess with success and try innovation, don't take a risk, and they become boring. So I like to do just exactly that, try and get different effects and use different styles to suit the drawing itself. The more you can vary your vocabulary, the better.

**HK:** So what makes a great cartoon? What are the characteristics that make you say "this is a great drawing"?

**PO:** Just a feeling of satisfaction with it, knowing you've done the best you can, you can't think of anything you'd change. That doesn't happen very often. You can see it immediately when it happens. These are all done with a fair amount of speed. I'm looking for the magic combination of the message and the drawing just melding perfectly. And maybe once every few years that happens to my satisfaction. I can always see what I've done wrong. I'm always learning. I'm the perennial student. And I don't think there's more than half-a-dozen cartoons that I've been really truly happy with in all the time I've been doing it. Some days you feel like this is really going well. You can tell. Other days, you're just drawing like a farmer and you don't know why. So it's a day-to-day thing, and you never know how it's going to turn out because you've got to do it on deadline. You can't do it on a whim. I can't take a day off. I have to get it done.

**HK:** Does it also depend on the issue that you're working with? Is it a combination of a lot of different elements?

**PO:** For any cartoon, you've got to care about the issue, or you don't do it. And then you've got to find the way it should be done. Will it be whimsical? Will it be heavy with a lot of bold black areas? Will it be done with a brush, or will it be penwork, which will give you a more whimsical feel.

**'I was about to say that if ol' J. Edgar was still running things, we wouldn't be having this big image problem … but let it pass.'**

May 11, 1995
Ink and white out over pencil on layered paper, 11⁹⁄₁₆ x 15¹⁄₁₆ in.

The Justice Department agreed to censure the acting deputy director of the Federal Bureau of Investigation, Larry A. Potts, for managerial failures during a 1992 siege of a white supremacist's cabin in Idaho which resulted in three deaths. The censure, the mildest of disciplinary actions, had been recommended by FBI Director Louis J. Freeh, who had reprimanded twelve FBI agents and suspended and reassigned two field commanders in January 1995 for their participation in the raid on Randall C. Weaver's cabin. On February 9, PBS's Frontline aired a documentary, *The Secret File on J. Edgar Hoover*, that included a segment about J. Edgar Hoover's alleged cross-dressing.

**HK:** If history records you as one of the great comic draftsmen, is that enough or is there more that you think you're bringing to the work now that you'd like to have . . . ?

**PO:** Well, it's my work in general I'd like to be known for, and not just in this area alone.

**HK:** Your sculptures and your paintings . . . .

**PO:** And everything, yes. I'd like it all to be remembered. I think the sculpture's got a fair chance of being well thought of.

**HK:** What was the ultimate goal of your reassessment? What did you think you were hoping to accomplish or create?

**PO:** A body of work, I guess. I'm trying to learn to accord my drawings the same respect I would expect other people to accord them. I had not yet met my wife, Susan Conway, who has a museum and conservation background and who taught me that you must treat these things with respect, not stick them in a corner and neglect them, which had been my usual way, because they are worth saving. It was Susan, also, who began getting the work placed in libraries and museums as bodies of work. Previously, I had sold them off piecemeal or carelessly given them away. I always vaguely hoped that they would be adopted by the Library of Congress, museums, other libraries. And so, on Susan's wise insistence, I have not sold or given away any cartoons singly for the past ten years. I had come to the realization I should be passing these drawings along. I have no idea how to teach this business, but, one day, people looking at these works may be able to get something from them. So, a little bit of hearing the clock ticking, thinking that I want them to have good homes one of these days.

**HK:** Well, go into that a little bit. Is it important for the Library of Congress to be collecting this material? What does it mean to you to see your work included in the collections?

**PO:** Now, you talk about awards, this is the award I like. And you were asking what would be a good alternative to Pulitzers and the like. The greatest award is to be part of a great collection such as this at the Library of Congress. I mean, this is the center of things. And to be in these collections is, to me, every award I could possibly want.

**HK:** These collections, as you know, are quite comprehensive, and have a lot of the great masters from past times. For me, one of the things that I get out of this job is the idea of developing these collections of political, and often controversial, art in the shadow of the U.S. Capitol. The Library functions as both the national library and a symbol of democracy.

**[Powell]**

July 11, 1996
Ink and white out over pencil on paper,
11¹/₁₆ x 14 in.

Having succeeded in his bid to become the Republican presidential nominee, Bob Dole was criticized on July 10 by retired General Colin L. Powell, whom he was heavily courting as a vice-presidential running mate, for failing to attend the NAACP convention. The former chairman of the Joint Chiefs of Staff was at a peak of visibility and popularity with the recent publication of his autobiography, *My American Journey.*

'I WANT TO BUILD A BRIDGE!' SAID ONE.
'A BRIDGE?' SAID THE OTHER, 'TO WHERE?'
'A BRIDGE TO THE TWENTY FIRST CENTURY.'
SAID THE FIRST.
'AH!' SAID THE OTHER, 'SO DO I!'
THEN THEY SAID, 'THAT'S A VERY LONG WAY.
LET'S JUST BUILD BRIDGES TO NOVEMBER.'
AND THEY DID.

There are a lot of countries where political cartoonists don't enjoy the freedom of expression you do, would never have access to a public institution like this one, and certainly their work would never be shown on its walls.

**PO:** Those are the reasons I'm so happy to be here. The fact that there is a Constitution, and we're protected under that Constitution in exercising the right of free speech. It's a wonderful thing. You've got to come from somewhere else to realize how valuable it is. Even in the so-called liberal democracies, like Britain and Australia, it's not the same. In a lot of European so-called democracies, this country is looked upon as a bomb-throwing radical. And to export this sort of democracy to Russia, for instance, I don't think they're completely ready for this sort of thing, this absolute freedom of speech. They believe in some control and some restriction.

**HK:** Except, as we've been saying, there are some very serious assaults on freedom of speech today with political correctness.

**PO:** Oh, there always are. There have always been threats to the freedom of speech in this country.

**HK:** What would you tell people? You know, you have a chance to really say to your readers what it is they should be grateful for.

**PO:** Well, that's what we're talking about. I am exercising here a great freedom of speech. Shut up and pay attention. [Laughter]

**HK:** Where else could they get this kind of opinion? Is there another way that they could get the kind of opinion that you express in your cartoons?

**PO:** Apparently not. I mean, I don't see it right now. Maybe there are certain stand-up comedians who can do this. But it's not something you can hold tangibly in your hand and say, "Look at that." Cut it out of the paper and contemplate for awhile. Go back and look at it again. It will look different. Go back again, it will look different again.

**HK:** Is the idea to create a body of work, with real paper and real ink, that will last for generations?

**PO:** Yes. I can't see it being done any other way than exactly that. On paper, with the drawings preserved and handled in a proper manner, in, of all places, the Library of Congress. It's a great honor to be part of that. And it's so good for the profession, to have people be accepted into that pantheon and have their work stored and displayed in such a way. It's good for the profession and it promotes it as an art, which is what I believe it to be.

**HK:** Well, we've talked a little bit about the traditions of cartooning. What do you think you bring to the collection? What do you think people will take from your work that they might not find elsewhere?

**PO:** Oh, I don't know. That's up to them. I don't know what they're looking for. But I hope students of cartooning would be interested in what I thought and how I approached an idea, how I drew it. How I wanted it to balance with the message. And I hope I've achieved that in a few cases, or at least that they will be able to see the struggle I went through daily to achieve that.

**HK:** Are there things you think you do particularly well?

**PO:** I put the drawing on equal footing with the idea. Or I can say that both are primary. They are both the most important thing. And I don't know how many people are doing that, paying attention to drawing. Students of cartooning may learn how to diversify their drawing styles so they don't get stuck. If they look at my earlier work and then my later work, they'll get some message that I would want them to get, that you must change your style all the time, it must be a living thing. And it should always be treated that way. It's like building a house, or anything else. One has to always learn. And like I said, I don't know whether I have more than half a dozen drawings that I'm really pleased with.

**HK:** Apart from the art, is there an attitude that you bring or a viewpoint that's going to be enduring and might also be a lesson to students of cartooning? Do you think you push the envelope in terms of your commentary a little more than most?

**PO:** Sure. You know, my syndicate is run by a wonderful bunch of guys but they're all Catholics, which is not their fault, and they're all from Notre Dame, which is also not their fault, and they're all fairly convinced that way, and what am I doing hanging out with this bunch? So I always gain great ancillary delight when I draw cartoons critical of the latest conservative papal dogma, knowing they will be groaning, "Oh, geez, what are you doing to us now?" Then they'll always gather up and defend me against the hailstorm which ensues, bless 'em.

**HK:** Well, let's talk about the syndicate and the future of the profession.

**[Dole and Clinton: the pot calling the kettle black]**

October 30, 1996
Ink and white out over pencil on paper,
10⅚ x 14 in.

A poll published on October 22, 1996, revealed that 63 percent of Americans thought that Dole spent more time attacking Clinton than explaining what his policies as president would be. Dole attacked Clinton's ethics and said of the White House at an October 27 Republican gathering, "It's the animal house!"

AND VICE VERSA, YOUR CHOICE

**PO:** Right now we're in a transition, the whole art is in a transition. Technology's changing. I am so pleased that this collection will go into the Library of Congress and be preserved as drawings on paper. It won't be a stack of floppy disks. I don't know where it's all going. I find that the quality of reproduction on the Internet is far better than you get in most newspapers. And I'm sure technology will even improve over that. So, with the modems speeding up and technology heading on at such a huge speed, you don't know what next year will bring. Against this, you have massive newspapers of incredible wealth investing huge sums in the latest technology, computers, satellite connections, etc., and printing their end product on fifty-year-old presses. It's like digitizing the buggy whip.

**HK:** Do you see positives to the Internet?

**PO:** If there were such a thing as a magazine or something like a publication on the Internet.

**HK:** But you wouldn't like to have an Oliphant Web site just devoted to your cartoons?

**PO:** I don't know what good it would do. Will anybody sit down to look at them on computers? Who's got the time any more to do that? It takes a long time to call up an image on the computer. Even if it was lightning-fast, would people bother? But they do have time, I hope, to look at a cartoon on a printed page. At this stage, I just don't know what it's going to be like. Here we are at the end of an era. We're going into something else now. I suppose the drawing on paper will be with us for a long time, but the audience now is hard to define. We're going off into the electronic world. I'm a traditionalist, in that I like the paper and drawing itself. I wouldn't like to work on a computer, for instance. You'd have no drawing in the end that you could put towards a body of work. Potentially, it's a wonderful audience, though, I mean it's worldwide. A far bigger audience and far better reproduction than you can get any other way. But I prefer working this way because it's what I'm used to.

**HK:** Why do people need to see the original work?

**PO:** Original drawing is a presence that no other form of copying is going to provide. I'm always awed when I'm in the presence of, say, a Charles Dana Gibson drawing. Just looking at it and seeing it. I don't know if that happens to everybody, but certain students and closer observers of the art are going to be pleased to be able to look at an original and feel that the artist was here. Right here. And, hopefully, with these comments, they'll be able to understand how I felt about it all. So, to me, it's a great service to my art to have the drawings where interested parties can have access to them.

**[Hear the amazing Al Gore explanation machine]**

August 28, 1997
Ink and white out over pencil on paper,
11 x 14 in.

Vice President Al Gore's fundraising telephone calls were top news during the week of August 24, 1997. A *Washington Post* article on August 27 reported that the forty-six people contacted by Gore contributed, directly or through their companies, almost $3.7 million in unregulated 'soft money' to the Democratic National Committee. At a news conference called to answer the allegations that he had broken federal law by making fundraising phone calls from federal property, Gore asserted that there was "no controlling legal authority" to decide the issue of campaign phone calls. In April, Gore had attended a fundraiser at a Buddhist temple in California, where it was alleged that at least one illegal donation had been made.

## Influence

September 19, 1997
Ink and white out over pencil on paper,
11 1/16 x 14 in.

The *Washington Post* and the *Los Angeles Times* reported in August and September 1997 that major Democratic campaign donors were gaining the ear of President Clinton in return for their money. During this period, videotapes were released under subpoena by the White House which showed Clinton and Gore socializing there with major campaign donors. The tapes confirmed the allegations by the newspapers that some of these donors were Asian-born or leaders of major companies doing business in Asia. Clinton and Gore are shown dressed as Buddhist monks in reference to a fundraiser attended by Gore at a Buddhist temple in California, whose legality was questioned. The message on the wall refers to alleged intercedings with the White House by a CIA official identified only as Bob, on behalf of a donor with questionable motives.

**HK:** I chose the title for the exhibition when I saw your oil painting called "Anthem." It's a very positive image of everybody working or singing together, different voices but the *same* voice. You've got thousands of drawings and thirty years of American history, Reagan and Clinton, all these Americans and all these themes played out in your work—and you're the conductor. It seems that there's at once an embrace of American culture and society and, at the same time, you're maintaining your own critical sense and perspective. Can you talk about that?

**PO:** You make the painting sound like an old Soviet poster exhorting the Omsk Farmers Collective to produce more. It's an affectionate thing. To feel part of the country, to give back to the country for being so welcomed and accepted, for America being able to realize what I was trying to do with my early work. I didn't realize it at the time because I was just drawing cartoons. I thought, looking back, "This is a bit cheeky, coming into a new country and criticizing it." But people didn't mind. It gave them a fresh look at things, and I don't know if there's another country in the world where you'd find that. People in those other countries would be up in arms and want to throw you back to where you came from.

**HK:** There are a lot of people who would say that your body of work is overwhelmingly negative . . . .

**PO:** And a lot of good people would call me cantankerous!

**HK:** I can't imagine whom! But, to my mind, and I think this is part of the nature of your profession—at least for some of the best people in your profession—you're getting up every day, yes, you do produce negative commentary on issues but, in essence, you're feeling very positive that you can make a difference, that you can educate people, that you can, in a positive way, point out when we might be going down the wrong road.

**PO:** You say this very well. I mean, you're saying everything that I think about in the dead of night. Just say it that way. It's hard for an artist to just come out and say these things. It's a nice thing to say and I agree with it wholeheartedly. And I'm glad you picked up on that painting, because, you know, I just started painting their faces, letting the paint lead me, and then I had a canvas full of open-mouthed faces who seemed to be singing. For some reason, I put the flag in afterwards, removing some faces to do so, because I thought it needed some other element. And then, when that was done, I wrote "Anthem" across the bottom. It was one of those paintings that grows, as a painting should, until it's finished. Maybe it's finished.

# Works in Other Media

**The Flimflam Man
(Bill Clinton),** 1996

Charcoal on paper, 92 x 80 in.
Collection of the artist.
Courtesy of Susan Conway Gallery,
Washington, DC

**The Ancient One,** 1994

Monotype, 30 x 22 in.
Collection of the artist.
Courtesy of Susan Conway Gallery,
Washington, DC

**Los Hermanos Penitentes,**
1994

Monotype, 30 x 22 in.
Collection of the artist.
Courtesy of Susan Conway Gallery,
Washington, DC

**Military Dance,** 1986

Wax, 11½ x 9½ x 6¾ in.
Collection of the artist.
Courtesy of Susan Conway Gallery,
Washington, DC

**Tip O'Neill,** 1985

Bronze, 6½ x 6½ x 7 in.
Collection of the artist.
Courtesy of Susan Conway Gallery,
Washington, DC

**Patrick Moynihan –
A Senator,** 1991

Bronze, 18½ x 6½ x 5 in.
Collection of the artist.
Courtesy of Susan Conway
Gallery, Washington, DC

**The Fixer (Clark Clifford),**
1991

Bronze, 23 x 19 x 9 in.
Collection of the artist.
Courtesy of Susan Conway Gallery,
Washington, DC

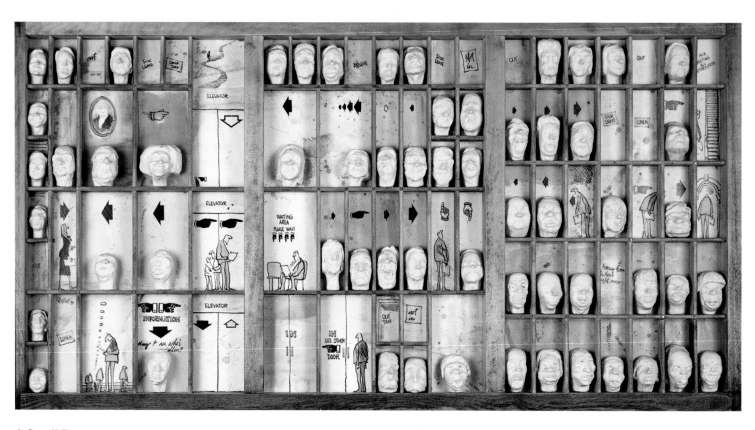

**A Small Bureaucracy,**
1983–1985

Mixed media sculpture,
16½ x 32 x 1⅜ in.
Collection of the artist.
Courtesy of Susan Conway Gallery,
Washington, DC

**Anthem,** 1997

Oil on canvas, 36 x 36 in.
Collection of the artist.
Courtesy of Susan Conway Gallery,
Washington, DC

## Exhibition Checklist

All cartoons and drawings
© Copyright Pat Oliphant

All objects in the exhibition are in the collections of the Prints and Photographs Division, Library of Congress, unless otherwise noted.

CARTOONS

*"They won't get us to the conference table . . . will they?"* February 1, 1966
Ink over pencil with paste-ons on duoshade paper, 11 13/16 × 17 5/8 in.
LC-USZ62-120078
(illustrated on p. 39)

*'. . . But first, let's hear your position on the Alaska pipeline and independent gas distributors!'* June 5, 1973
Ink over pencil with paste-ons on duoshade paper, 11 5/8 × 17 5/8 in.
LC-USZ62-120039
(illustrated on p. 15)

*'Politics is hell, Bebe!'* August 29, 1973
Ink over pencil with paste-on on duoshade paper, 11 9/16 × 17 9/16 in.
LC-USZ62-120047
(illustrated on p. 16)

*'Amateur!'* June 9, 1974
Ink over pencil with paste-on on duoshade paper, 11 9/16 × 17 9/16 in.
LC-USZ62-120048
(illustrated on p. 18)

*'First of all . . . Merry Christmas!'*
October 27, 1974
Ink over pencil with paste-on on duoshade paper, 11 9/16 × 17 5/8 in.
LC-USZ62-120070
(illustrated on p. 19)

*'May I please have your undivided attention . . ?'* November 13, 1974
Ink and white out over pencil with paste-on on duoshade paper, 11 9/16 × 17 5/8 in.
LC-USZ62-120049
(illustrated on p. 21)

*'If this is the only safe thing we can do to get back on the front pages, then I say let's do it!'* December 12, 1979
Ink over pencil on duoshade paper, 11 3/8 × 17 1/4 in.
LC-USZ62-120051
(illustrated on p. 22)

*'Whatever you say, Imam—I guess you know what you're doing . . .'*
April 24, 1980
Ink and white out over pencil on duoshade paper, 11 1/4 × 17 1/4 in.
LC-USZ62-120069
(illustrated on p. 24)

*'Everything is under control—go back to your designated shanties and slums!'*
June 20, 1980
Ink and brush over pencil on duoshade paper, 11 1/4 × 17 1/4 in.
LC-USZ62-120068
(illustrated on p. 25)

*'Hold steady, men—our show of unity seems to have them bamboozled!'*
December 17, 1980
Ink, brush, and white out over pencil on duoshade paper, 11 9/16 × 17 in.
LC-USZ62-120052
(illustrated on p. 27)

*'Sandra O'Connor, how plead you to the heinous charge of secular womanism?'* September 10, 1981
Ink over pencil on duoshade paper, 11 1/2 × 17 9/16 in.
LC-USZ62-120050
(illustrated on p. 28)

*'Sí, Presidente Duarte, you can tell them in Washington that El Salvador continues to move steadily towards democracy.'* September 24, 1981
Ink over pencil on duoshade paper, 11 9/16 × 17 5/8 in.
LC-USZ62-120079
(illustrated on p. 31)

*Alliance for some sort of progress*
February 26, 1982
Ink and white out over pencil on layered paper, 11 1/4 × 17 1/2 in.
LC-USZ62-120055
(illustrated on p. 32)

*Watchdog,* December 21, 1982
Ink over pencil on layered paper, 11 1/4 × 17 in.
LC-USZ62-120062
(illustrated on p. 35)

*[U.S. Embassy—Business as usual]*
April 20, 1983
Ink over pencil on layered paper, 11 1/4 × 17 1/2 in.
LC-USZ62-120045
(illustrated on p. 36)

*There he goes again,* February 8, 1984
Ink over pencil on layered paper, 11 3/16 × 17 1/2 in.
LC-USZ62-120063
(illustrated on p. 40)

*Let a thousand flowers bloom*
March 25, 1986
Ink and white out over pencil on layered paper, 11 5/16 × 17 9/16 in.
LC-USZ62-120043
(illustrated on p. 42)

*[Watch my lips—I'm gonna be the environment president!]*
December 7, 1988
Ink and white out over pencil on paper, 11 1/2 × 17 1/16 in.
LC-USZ62-120044
(illustrated on p. 43)

*[Destitute S&L please help]*
January 13, 1989
Ink and white out on paper, 11 1/2 × 17 1/16 in.
LC-USZ62-120041
(illustrated on p. 44)

*Remember Tiananmen Square*
June 5, 1989
Ink, brush and white out over pencil on layered paper board, 11 9/16 × 17 9/16 in.
LC-USZ62-120042
(illustrated on p. 47)

*'Hold it . . . wait for me!'*
August 23, 1989
Ink, brush and white out over pencil on layered paper, 11 11/16 × 17 1/2 in.
LC-USZ62-120053
(illustrated on p. 48)

*'Tis the season to be jolly, my good man! We won—did you know that? Capitalism is triumphant. Communism lies in ruins. Our system prevails! We won! Smile!'* December 8, 1989
Ink and white out over pencil on layered paper, 11 9/16 × 17 1/2 in.
LC-USZ62-120040
(illustrated on p. 51)

[Fidel Castro building a sand castle]
January 10, 1990
Ink and white out over pencil on
layered paper, 11⅝ × 17⁹⁄₁₆ in.
LC-USZ62-120031
(illustrated on p. 52)

'How cozy it is on these cold winter
evenings, to snuggle down in front of TV
and watch the war.' January 22, 1991
Ink and white out over pencil on
paper, 11⁹⁄₁₆ × 17¹⁄₁₆ in.
LC-USZ62-120036
(illustrated on p. 54)

'Oo! Is it too late to go back to
sanctions?' February 14, 1991
Ink and white out over pencil on paper,
11⁹⁄₁₆ × 17 in.
LC-USZ62-120033
(illustrated on p. 55)

[Jesse Helms attacks cultural funding]
March 6, 1992
Ink and white out over pencil on
layered paper, 11½ × 17½ in.
LC-USZ62-120030
(illustrated on p. 56)

The Democratic field at this time
March 19, 1992
Ink and white out over pencil on paper
11½ × 17¹⁄₁₆ in.
LC-USZ62-120029
(illustrated on p. 59)

[Free at last!], April 30, 1992
Ink and white out over pencil on paper,
11½ × 17 in.
LC-USZ62-120034
(illustrated on p. 60)

[Howdy! I'm Ross Perot and I'm
running for president], June 1, 1992
Ink and white out over pencil on
layered paper board, 11⁹⁄₁₆ × 17¹⁄₁₆ in.
Swann Fund Purchase
LC-USZ62-120032
(illustrated on p. 63)

'Either all our chickens came home to
roost, or this is the Arkansas transition
team.' November 6, 1992
Ink and white out over pencil on paper,
11⅝ × 17 in.
LC-USZ62-120065
(illustrated on p. 64)

It's reveille in America!
February 18, 1993
Ink and white out over pencil on paper,
11½ × 16¹⁵⁄₁₆ in.
Swann Fund Purchase
LC-USZ62-119294, LC-USZC4-5591
(illustrated on p. 65)

Nine lives and counting . . .
March 25, 1993
Ink and white out over pencil on paper,
11½ × 17¹⁄₁₆ in.
LC-USZ62-120046
(illustrated on p. 67)

'Thank you for not interfering.'
April 15, 1993
Ink and white out over pencil
on paper, 11⁹⁄₁₆ × 17 in.
LC-USZ62-120054
(illustrated on p. 68)

[I won't ask! Don't ask! I mustn't ask!
Don't ask! I can't ask! Don't ask! So
don't ask! Don't ask!], July 10, 1993
Ink and white out over pencil on
paper, 11½ × 17 in.
LC-USZ62-120037
(illustrated on p. 71)

[Rabin, Arafat, and dove of peace]
September 14, 1993
Ink and white out over pencil on
paper, 11⁹⁄₁₆ × 17¹⁄₁₆ in.
Swann Fund Purchase
LC-USZ62-120067
(illustrated on p. 72)

'Now, tell the jury what you did with
the knife, Mrs. Bobbitt . . .'
January 12, 1994
Ink and white out over pencil on
paper, 11⁷⁄₁₆ × 16¹⁵⁄₁₆ in.
LC-USZ62-120074
(illustrated on p. 75)

[Richard Nixon holding up his arms
with the victory symbol]
April 23, 1994
Ink and white out over pencil on
layered paper, 11½ × 17 in.
Swann Fund Purchase
LC-USZ62-120072
(illustrated on pp. 12–13)

RMN. Lest we forget, April 28, 1994
Ink and white out over pencil on
layered paper, 11½ × 17 in.
LC-USZ62-120073
(illustrated on p. 76)

[Sit down, whoy don't you? If you'll sit
down, then oi'll sit down, then we'll be
all sittin' down], September 2, 1994
Ink and white out over pencil on
paper, 11⁹⁄₁₆ × 15¾ in.
LC-USZ62-120071
(illustrated on p. 81)

'I've got an idea for '96 – I go back, I
beg forgiveness, play the whole
redemption bit, the reformed underdog
back from hell, I get re-elected, we
take over . . .' September 17, 1994
Ink and white out on paper,
11½ × 15⅜ in.
LC-USZ62-120060
(illustrated on p. 79)

Off to the revolution, January 6, 1995
Ink and white out over pencil on
paper, 11⁹⁄₁₆ × 15¹⁄₁₆ in.
Swann Fund Purchase
LC-USZ62-120058
(illustrated on p. 83)

'You may be the commanding general
of Post 17 of the Grand Patriot Militia,
but in this outfit you're the private
who takes the garbage to the dump!'
April 28, 1995
Ink and tonal film overlay on paper,
11⅝ × 15¹⁄₁₆ in.
LC-USZ62-120076
(illustrated on p. 91)

'I was about to say that if ol' J. Edgar
was still running things, we wouldn't
be having this big image problem . . .
but let it pass.' May 11, 1995
Ink and white out over pencil on
layered paper, 11⁹⁄₁₆ × 15¹⁄₁₆ in.
LC-USZ62-120038
(illustrated on p. 92)

'It's no good—I am who I am.'
February 22, 1996
Ink and white out over pencil on
paper, 11 × 14 in.
Swann Fund Purchase
LC-USZ62-120059
(illustrated on p. 6)

[Powell], July 11, 1996
Ink and white out over pencil on
paper, 11¹¹⁄₁₆ × 14 in.
LC-USZ62-120066
(illustrated on p. 95)

['I want to build a bridge!' said one.]
October 21, 1996
Ink and white out over pencil on
paper, 11¹⁄₁₆ × 14¹⁄₁₆ in.
LC-USZ62-120056
(illustrated on p. 96)

[Dole and Clinton: the pot calling the
kettle black], October 30, 1996
Ink and white out over pencil on
paper, 10⅝ × 14 in.
LC-USZ62-120077
(illustrated on p. 99)

[Mir Missionkontrol], August 20, 1997
Ink and white out over pencil on
paper, 10¹⁵⁄₁₆ × 14 in.
LC-USZ62-120035
(illustrated on p. 100)

[Hear the amazing Al Gore explanation
machine], August 28, 1997
Ink and white out over pencil on
paper, 11 × 14 in.
Swann Fund Purchase
LC-USZ62-120075
(illustrated on p. 102)

Influence, September 19, 1997
Ink and white out over pencil on
paper, 11¹⁄₁₆ × 14 in.
Swann Fund Purchase
LC-USZ62-120064
(illustrated on p. 103)

[Budget Shell Game]
February 10, 1997
Ink and white out over pencil on
paper, 11 × 14 in.
LC-USZ62-120061
(illustrated on p. 105)

# Socks Goes to Washington

SOCKS GOES TO WASHINGTON.

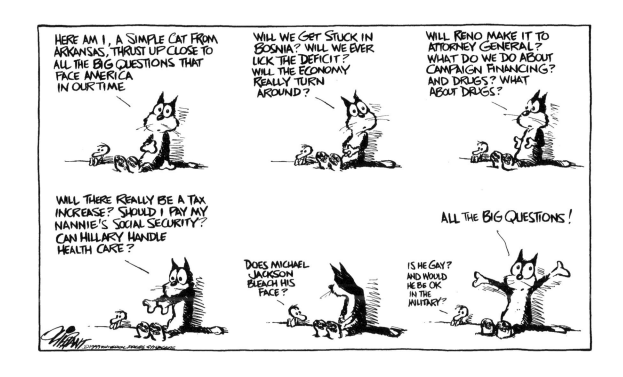

## To read more about Pat Oliphant:

James Stevenson, "Profiles: Endless Possibilities," *The New Yorker*, December 31, 1979, 38–46.

Wayne King, "What's So Funny about Washington?" *The New York Times Magazine*, August 5, 1990.

Wendy Wick Reaves, *Oliphant's Presidents: Twenty-five Years of Caricature by Pat Oliphant*, a retrospective exhibition at the National Portrait Gallery, Smithsonian Institution, 1990 (Kansas City: Andrews McMeel Publishing, 1990).

*Oliphant: The New World Order in Drawing and Sculpture 1983–1993* (Kansas City: Andrews McMeel Publishing, 1994).

Wendy Wick Reaves, *Seven Presidents: The Art of Oliphant*, an exhibition at the San Diego Museum of Art, San Diego, California, 1995 (San Diego Museum of Art and Susan Conway Gallery, 1995).